Where It Was Hot

No more the sound of engine roar
with pulsing, throbbing din...
The fire is out, the job is done,
The All Out now is in...
No more the striking bells will call
there is a battle to be fought...
No more to face the smoke and flame,
To serve, to serve
Where it was hot.

Where It Was
HOT

by

Connie O'Brien

dmc associates
Dover, NH

Dedication

I respectfully dedicate this book to all firefighters who have given their lives while serving their communities.

Author's Note

I suppose that many people think the fire service is a job of courage and horror. Having served with the Cambridge, MA Fire Department for over four decades, I will have to say this was and is essentially true. Firefighters have a dangerous job; they do witness tragedy regularly. To do this type of work does require a certain kind of courage.

However, there is another side to the job that runs parallel, and it is good that is does. This side is humor. I honestly believe that without humor it would be impossible for any person to remain a firefighter, to make a career of firefighting. Humor is what allows us to continue to deal with the tragedy we confront.

For many years my lovely wife and seven kids have been after me to write about my career with the Cambridge Fire Department. I finally decided to give it a try. I hope you enjoy the result, **Where It Was Hot**. I enjoyed recalling the funny incidents, all those good times. And while it is never pleasurable to recall tragic events, I do believe they should never be forgotten.

Connie O'Brien
Cambridge, MA
March 1998

Acknowledgments

I am certain that there are many former firefighters out there who have many stories. Perhaps they would tell those stories if they only had the proper support. I was very fortunate in the fact that such support was there for me, and I would like to thank the close friends and family members who helped make this book become a reality:

My sons, Michael, a fire captain, and Neal, a firefighter— both members of the City of Nashua, New Hampshire Fire Department.

My son, Stephen, an engineer with Digital Equipment Corporation.

My son, Timmy, a motorcycle officer with the City of Cambidge Police Department.

My son, Eugene, an electrician with a manufacturing company.

My daughter, Eileen, a paralegal and a happily married mother of three children.

My daughter, Jennifer, an aspiring actress.

My wife, Mary, who entered my liffe when I thought there were no more flowers in the garden.

My fellow firefighters, who are members of the select society called the "bravest of the brave."

Where It Was Hot

Part One

Cambridge, Mass.

Cambridge, Massachusetts is different than most cities in many ways. Within this compact municipality, consisting of 7.14 square miles, you can find nearly the entire spectrum of contemporary human society. The rich and the affluent societal bands are separated from each other by only a few miles. In the center of the city is Harvard University, with its many buildings dedicated to the pursuit of higher education. On the banks of the Charles River, across from the high towers of downtown Boston, the Massachusetts Institute of Technology (aka MIT) covers a massive twenty block area, a bee hive of high tech, cutting edge research and development, including atomic energy research.

In between and beyond these two institutions are the middle class and the poor. Many sections of the city contain block after block of third-class, wood frame, multiple occupancy dwellings. On a warm evening you could reach out an open kitchen window and shake hands with the next door neighbor without too much effort.

In the northwest section of the city there are high-rise apartment complexes, office buildings and an industrial area.

At the present time, Cambridge's population hovers in the vicinity of 98,000 people. Cambridge is a relatively healthy American city, largely due to the cosmopolitan and diverse nature of its population. It is surrounded by cities with similar types of construction and occupancy. Collectively these communities are known as the Metro Boston Area. Those municipalities closest to the "Hub" are the most densely populated.

The Cambridge Fire Department consists of nine engines, four of which are double units—hose wagon, pumper—and are considered a single engine company; four ladder companies are housed in various locations throughout the city. All share the same quarters as the engine companies. Two rescue units, a hazardous materials units, a command unit, and various unit vehicles are located at fire headquarters. Lighting and rehab units are operated by a well organized and staffed auxiliary department. The rehab unit is very necessary due to the new type of bunker gear the firefighters must wear. This unit provides a cool down area in the summer and a place to get out of the cold in the winter.

Cambridge is broken into two divisions, with Harvard Square serving as the divider. A deputy chief is in charge of each division. An additional chief is stationed at headquarters and is available if requested by the incident commander. Safety officers are assigned to respond to greater alarms. It is their duty to observe working conditions at an incident and to report structural weakness and other unsafe conditions to the command center.

A very sophisticated system of mutual aid is in place which can provide assistance within the Metro Fire District. Due to reduced manpower and numbers of fire stations in many cities and towns, mutual aid is vital for fire control. When a major fire occurs in a city within the Metro system, they will receive additional engine and ladder companies to assist them. Some of these units will respond directly to the fire; others will cover vacant stations.

The problem facing Cambridge in the last years of the 20th century are not unlike those of Greater Boston in general or any large metropolitan area in the United States. Change will come since no has yet found a way to prevent or slow down the passage of time. Besides, those who will not accept change will be changed by the concept that they refuse to accept.

Kendall Square

As a young boy I lived in a housing project in the Cambridge Port section of the city. This area runs along the Charles River near the Boston line. My father passed away in 1939 and we moved to Newtowne Court from North Cambridge. This was a new housing project for low income families. The apartment buildings of the Newtowne Court complex were surrounded by factories.

My mother worked washing dishes in Central Square to help support my two sisters and me. During the early years of the war I sold newspapers on Essex Street in Boston. I worked the bars and taverns where the sailors hung out, and the tips were very good. We usually settled up with Sammy, the newspaper dealer, about nine-thirty at night after the last edition of the Boston *Record American*. Sammy was a small, serious man who never failed to tell us to go directly home. To save money I would walk home to Cambridge, a distance of about two miles. My mother would get angry with me for not taking the subway. However, there were two methods to my madness.

First, I did want to save the subway fare money. But the second reason was the big one. Walking back to Cambridge allowed me to pass two fire stations. The first firehouse that I passed was Bowdoin Square. This was a very large Boston station and housed two engine companies, a rescue company, water tower, ladder truck and a division chief. There was always something doing at the Bowdoin Square station, and I would stand across the street and watch the almost constant activity.

After crossing over the West Boston bridge, I would come to

—4—

the next fire station—Cambridge Engine 7 in Kendall Square. This area was a factory district that contained such companies as Lever Brothers Soap, Boston Woven Hose, Deran Chocolates and various other manufacturers. Further down on Main Street were rows of tenement houses, and beyond that was the Newtowne Court housing project where I lived.

When I reached Engine 7, a two piece company, I was almost home. I always kept one paper in my bag for Mr. Campbell. He was a lieutenant at Engine 7 and knew what time I would be coming by. Many times he would invite me in for a cup of hot soup. I would sit happily at the kitchen table, eating my soup, listening to the conversations and sometimes saying a few words, little knowing that one day I would be the captain of that house.

One cold and rainy night, Lt. Campbell scolded me for not wearing a warmer coat. The next time he caught me with the same coat on, soaking wet after crossing the bridge in the rain, he really got mad and said that he would call my mother. This time I told him the truth, that I did not own another coat. He just stood there staring at me, not saying a word.

I wouldn't see Lt. Campbell every night, only when he was on duty. About four nights later he was standing out in front of the firehouse, waiting for me. When I finished my bowl of soup and crackers, all the firemen gathered around me and Lt. Campbell handed me a large flat box. When I opened the box, there it was, a brand new green winter coat. "Gee wiz, Mister Campbell, I can't take this!" I said. "All the boys in Group Seven got it for you," he replied, "and I've already called your mother about it."

I will always remember Mr. Campbell and the generosity of the firefighters in Group Seven.

Engine 7—Baggy Pants and Monkey Business

Sometimes when I was off school for the weekend or vacation, I would spend an afternoon with the boys at Engine 7. There was a guy named Harry who worked in Group Four. He was a tall skinny fellow and very good natured; Harry loved to laugh.

Engine 7's station was surrounded by factories. One block down the street was the Deran Candy factory. In a little plot of grass next to the fire station stood the only tree in the area and a picnic table, and in the summertime the girls from the candy factory would eat their lunch at this pastoral spot. They were a friendly bunch, always full of the devil.

Harry would wear a pair of baggy chino pants; he'd fill his pockets with bolts, washers and change. While the girls sat at the picnic table and ate their lunch, Harry would do a little soft shoe dance, which, of course, the girls would watch, and when he pulled in his stomach his pants would drop just as if someone had yanked them down, and there Harry stood, for all to see, wearing a pair of white boxers with large red hearts all over them. The girls would roar.

We even had a romance develop because of that bit of grass: Bob Clancy met his future bride there; she was one of the candy girls, dressed completely in white, even a white hair net.

The firefighters at Engine 7 enjoyed telling me stories of the old time firemen who had been stationed there. One story was about a captain who had a pet monkey. His wife's brother was a merchant seaman who brought the monkey back from one his trips and gave the exotic creature to her as a pet. I guess the monkey did not make much of a hit in their home because it ended up living in the firehouse.

One day the chief came into quarters for some reason, and the monkey stole his fine gold braided hat. Up into the hose tower raced the monkey. The captain was in the tower shaking the rope and yelling, "Come down, come down you goddam monkey and give the chief back his hat!" while the chief yelled at the captain for having the animal in the house. The men yelled, "Call a cop and shoot the monkey!" Apparently, *they* had to clean up after it. The monkey came down, started jumping from the hose wagon to the pumper, and ended up swinging from the overhead light, still clutching the unhappy chief's tattered hat.

It all resolved when the chief left quarters, bellowing that he had two hats and that he would return. The monkey tired of the sport and left what remained of the hat on the hose rack. The captain called his wife and blamed her for the whole mess.

The Animal Rescue took the monkey to his new home and the captain took up residence in his new home, the firehouse. His wife did not agree that it was her fault the chief had lost his hat.

A Question of Pride

When I joined the navy in 1946, my Irish mother gave me a kiss good-bye and told me to keep good company and never do a thing that I would not want her to see.

They were a proud lot, those Irish people; they had so much community pride. The area where we lived was primarily Irish, but it was also home to many Polish, Italian and French families. Each week the tenants who lived in the Newtowne Project would take turns washing the front stairs. Another tenant would wash the walls. This was done on a rotation system. A schedule was posted and everyone got a crack at the community's various domestic chores. Mr. Burnam, who lived on the first floor, would oversee the tasks. If you failed to initial in the appropriate box, there would be a knock at your door and Mr. Burnam would gently ask what the problem was. If there was a sickness in the house, he understood and that was the end of the matter.

Mr. Burnam was never paid. He was simply a classy guy who, like many of the people back then, had simple pride in his neighborhood. The morning I left for the navy he was standing at the foot of the stairs and shook hands with me. When I took my hand away, I was holding a five dollar bill.

The baby carriage brigade would walk up to Central Square to get A.D.C. (Aid to Dependent Children) milk. A vacant store was used to dispense the items they had to give that day. Bags of potatoes were dumped in a bin and you could fill one bag. Sometimes carrots were available. It bothered me to see my mother dig into that bin. Down Massachusetts Avenue they strolled, the baby carriage brigade—but there were no babies in the carriages, only food. It was always a question of pride.

For a time my mother took a job washing dishes and later became a cook in a department store in Central Square. When the day was over, she would ask Rose, the woman who was her boss, if she could buy the unused food. Rose always gave her the food and no money was ever accepted. Later on, my mother got me a job washing dishes—mainly to keep me out of trouble. I was really too young to work, but Mr. Brody paid me under the table. One day I was told to load up the potato peeler with potatoes. No one knew that somehow a rat had got inside the peeler, and when I started the damned machine the rat flew right over my head and scared the hell out of me.

We did not have much, but what we did have we appreciated. I do sometimes think that the major problem with people today is that in many cases they have too much. They have lost the ability to appreciate—perhaps because they have never been hungry. I will always remember the baby carriage brigade, however, as a symbol of both poverty and pride.

After returning from the service and working at various jobs, I finally achieved my goal, what I always longed for. I became a fireman. Naturally, someone blew the whistle and the Cambridge Housing Authority informed us that because I worked for the fire department, our income would disqualify us from living in Newtowne Court any longer. We had to move.

In later years as I walked among the burnt-out hallways of the housing project that was once my community, I thought of Mr. Burnam and how times have changed.

The Anticipation of Adventure

The night before I was scheduled to report for duty as a member of the Cambridge Fire Department, sleep was hard to come by. I had waited so long for this day. When the news reached me that Engine 5 in Inman Square would be my assignment, I was elated. This was a very busy engine company that was located in a congested tenement area. The incidence of fire was great. Hardly a day would pass without some kind of action.

Most of these tenement dwellings were without central heating and used range oil heaters in the kitchen and parlor. A fifty-five gallon drum of kerosene was usually stored in the basement or in some cases on the back porch. When the residents needed oil for the stove, they carried it in a three-gallon container up the back stairs. This container was attached to the back of the stove and provided fuel for the heater. Inevitably some of the oil would spill on the stairs and on the linoleum. The great problem was that when a fire started in the cellar, it found its way to the rear stairs and porches. When the flames found the oil soaked wood, they quickly headed for the sky. No matter how fast we arrived at the scene, the fire would beat us and vital means of egress was gone. We almost always had to use the front stairs, which quickly became untenable with smoke. We made many, many rescues over ladders because this was the only way out.

Engine 5 was on the border of Cambridge and Somerville and we responded to many of their line boxes. The neighborhood around Inman Square was Portuguese, Italian and Irish. All these people had one common element: they were all trying to do the best that they could and make a living.

Finally, my night of little sleep ended and the first day of my career as a Cambridge firefighter began. With great expectation, I reported for work at the quarters of Engine Company 5. It had been snowing all night and about seven inches of snow were already of the ground. The fire station was a large, imposing building with many doors; it seemed almost intimidating to me. Not yet issued a uniform, I stood awkwardly next to the patrol desk on the apparatus floor—twenty-one years old and rearing to go!

Lieutenant Malvern sat at the desk and addressed me: "Welcome, kid. Take a snow shovel and walk up Cambridge Street and every time you see a fat looking pipe sticking out of the sidewalk, shovel the devil out of it."

As I walked along the snow covered sidewalk and searched for half-hidden hydrants I thought to myself, "There must be more to the job than this!" There was, of course, much more...but all that was hidden from my view on that snowy winter morning.

The Horses

When I was stationed at Engine 5 in Inman Square, I met a few of the former firemen who had been on the job when horses pulled fire engines. One old timer, Mr. Flaherty, would sit near the door at the rear of the apparatus floor. This door led to the rear shop and hose storage area. Mr. Flaherty knew there would always be a breeze at this spot during the summer months. With both apparatus doors and the rear garage doors open, it was like a gentle wind tunnel there.

One day Mr. Flaherty and I were talking and he pointed to the floor. "See that pipe sticking out the floor there? That used to be the connection to the five pound steam line in the cellar. There was a quick connect shut-off valve there, and when we'd get a run it could be easily shut off.

"The coal fired boiler in the cellar was always on and hot water circulated through the steam pumper boiler," he further explained. "A constant temperature of near two hundred and twelve degrees was always kept in the engine boiler. When we had a run, the engineer riding at the rear of the pump would disconnect the hot water line, *strike match*—which meant ignite a fire under the steam boiler on the pumper—and before we reached Hampshire Street, black smoke was puffing from the stack.

"Then we'd connect the pump to the hydrant and the steam would furnish pressure to the hoses. When we got back from the run the engineer would *dump fire* and lay a new bed on the grates under the steamer. He used channel coal and waste soaked with kerosene oil. You see, son, this would ignite real quick."

He loved to talk about his good old days, and when I remember his stories I am so glad I took the time to listen. The steamer and the horses are gone for ever, and in many respects, the "romance" of firefighting is gone too. Mr. Flaherty brought those days a bit closer to me.

The horses were a specially loved subject to him. They were kept in the stable area at the rear of the station. Each horse had a stall. A horse seldom lies down since they can sleep on their feet. The harness equipment was suspended from the ceiling. If a run was for that station, the man on floor patrol would pull the stall door release rope. When the doors opened, the horses knew that it was a run for them. They would then trot forward and the driver would position them under the harnesses. The rope holding the harness equipment to the ceiling was pulled, and the staves and collars dropped over the horses. A man would snap the collars in place and throw the reins up to the driver.

The steam engineer, who rode the rear step, would disconnect the hot water line to the boiler. Engine 5 ran a hose tender and a pumping engine. This requires three horses on the pump and two on the hose tender. Spare horses were kept in the stable in the rear. On a particularly busy night the horses would be changed frequently. When they arrived at the fire, the horses were taken from the scene. These animals could not tolerate smoke very well. The driver would take them up the street as far as possible away from the smoke.

I especially remember one incident Mr. Flaherty shared with me. An alarm came in for a fire in an East Cambridge factory. Engine 5 responded. When the driver snapped the collar around the horse's neck, something went wrong and the horse's head was turned sharply to one side. This seriously effected the animal's ability to breathe. The driver, realizing that the horse was in trouble, tried to stop the engine, but the horse knew that he was on his way to a fire and refused to slow down. Since he was the lead horse, the other horses kept right on pulling.

When they finally arrived at the fire, the animal dropped dead. Later the veterinarian said that he had run while he was choking to death; the vet couldn't understand how the horse had made it. Mr. Flaherty said that there were more people around that horse than there were at the fire.

The animals were both loyal and smart. When the bells started ringing, they would react. The opening of the stall door was their signal to spring into action. During busy nights, the horses were replaced with fresh ones from the stable out back. Mr. Flaherty told me about one Fourth of July night when the same box was being struck continuously for false alarms. Eventually that lead horse knew that he was not going to an actual fire and there was simply no way he was going to run. On the way back to the firehouse, however, he would run like the devil was chasing him.

On Sunday mornings the driver would take the stable horses for a gallop up and down the street. If an alarm came in during this exercise, the man on floor watch would pull the cord to the bell in the hose tower. When the driver heard the bell, he would run the horses back to the station.

Mr. Flaherty also told me there were incidents when horses would tangle with motor cars. The animal always lost. As he spoke to me I could see his eyes sparkle as he remembered the old days. When he spoke of their passing, a tear ran down his cheek. Motor power won out. It was the end of an era.

Retired fire horses could not be used for any work around the city where they might hear a bell or a siren. They would rear up and take off after the engines. This response was the cause of many unpleasant accidents. The horses were loyal and true public servants who never failed to do their duty. They were also a vital part of the romance of firefighting.

The Spittoon

Shortly after being appointed, I was informed of my house duties. A spittoon squatted on the second floor near the window overlooking the square. One of my jobs was to clean the spittoon every morning that I was on duty. This task disgusted me and I vowed that I would find a way to ditch the job. An older, retired firefighter who sat at the window ever day looking down at the street was really the spittoon's sole user. I decided to hide the damned thing and maybe everyone would forget about it.

The next day my old friend came upstairs as usual, took his customary seat and began reading his paper. As I swept the floor I watched his reaction. He had a chew in his mouth big enough to choke a mule. He glanced out the window and then down where the pot should be and slowly shook his head, saying, "Sonny, there is something missing here and if we don't find it in a hurry, two things are going to happen—both very unpleasant."

I never learned what those unpleasant consequences were because I promptly produced the spittoon.

His name was Tom and he too had been on the job when horses pulled the engines to fires. Sometimes as he sat at his place by the window, I would come up behind him and sing "I'll Take you Home Again, Kathleen" and tears would run down his cheeks and out came the bandanna handkerchief to blow his nose. Tom never asked me to sing, but whenever I did he had the same reaction.

A Bagful of Doughnuts

When I reported for duty, a greasy brown paper bag of doughnuts was always placed on the fireplace mantel. The doughnuts were always as hard as bricks, but if you soaked them in some hot coffee they were palatable. Many times I'd be running late and would leave the house for work without eating dinner. The bag of doughnuts was always faithfully there and tasted pretty good in a growling, empty stomach. Many a night I would sit at the kitchen table after returning from a run at three o'clock in the morning and wonder who our house's Good Samaritan was as I dunked and dunked and munched.

One summer day I was working on the roof, laying out hose to dry, when I noticed an old man walking into the yard at the rear of the doughnut shop. I recognized him as one of the senior set who would hang in front of the station. As I watched in amazement, the silver-haired gent took a greasy, brown paper bag from his back pocket and proceeded to fill it with doughnuts he removed from the rubbish barrel. He paid no attention to the rats that jumped out after being disturbed.

My mouth hung open in shock as I looked down the stairs to the apparatus floor and saw him hand the bag to the man of floor patrol, saying, "Here are the doughnuts for the boys." Needless to say that after thanking the man we told him, "NO MORE DOUGHNUTS! We're putting on too much weight, old friend."

Apparently, the old gent had been providing the doughnuts for years before I was appointed; no one ever questioned his source. They were doughnuts! They were free! My doughnut discovery also explained the little teeth marks in the doughnuts. I always said to the guys, "Someone is taking a bite and if they don't like it they put it back."

Well, I was partially correct.

Macarelli's

Occasionally we were feeling flush or no one felt like cooking, so we would send out for lunch. East Cambridge had many good Italian restaurants, but Macarelli's, located on Warren Street, was our favorite spot. It wasn't a fancy place, but the food was very good and inexpensively priced, which is always an advantage. They also took telephone orders. They did not, however, make deliveries. We had five men on duty, but since I was "the boot"—the new recruit—I was selected to pick up the food.

One waitress who worked at Macarelli's was a real big gal; I think she drove trucks on the side. She was about 5'7" and weighed in at about 180 pounds. If it was busy when I got to the restaurant, she would make me stand and wait until she was good and ready to attend to a take-out order. If I said anything to her, she would start yelling: "Who the hell do you firemen think you are? You wait you goddam turn!"

One day she forgot to put the bread into the bag and I had to go back to the restaurant. Half of Macarelli's was used as a bar, and when I returned she was tending the bar. I told her as gently as I could that she forgot the bread and then all hell broke loose. "You want that I should come down there and eat the goddam spaghetti for you." I should have stood up to her, but—remember—she was a woman; she was also bigger than I. I picked up a loaf of scalli bread at the bakery next door.

Another time I was off duty and decided to have dinner at

Macarelli's. There she was, as big as life, maybe bigger, standing behind the counter. I sat at a booth. When my pasta came it was really heaped onto the plate, a very generous serving. Each table had a glass container of hot red pepper and I decided that a dash of the pepper on the pasta would be a nice touch. Unfortunately, some wise guy had loosened the cap, the red pepper rushed out of the shaker and my pasta dinner was ruined.

There I sat, a large plate of food that was too spicey to eat. She must have been watching me. Over she came, hands on her hips, and in a voice that people up on Cambridge Street could hear she said, "Well, it looks like you screwed that up!" I just smiled and asked for the check. In a few minutes she returned to the table, placed a fresh plate of pasta before me and said, "Easy on the hot stuff, baby." Then she looked both ways to see if anyone was looking and gave me a smile that I will never forget.

Sometime later we had three alarm fire in a tenement block down the street from Macarelli's. The fire broke out in the late evening. We had answered a false alarm about eight blocks away. When we got the call to respond to Warren Street, it took a while to get out of the street and rolling. Normally we would have been first due engine company on the scene.

When we got there the place was really sailing. It was Saturday night. The guy who lived on the first floor was a painter and when he came home he just stuffed all his drop cloths and painting equipment under the front stairs. We determined later that when he left the barroom and came home he must have accidentally dropped a match in the front hall after he lit a cigarette. The fire wasted no time running the stairs all the way up to the fourth floor. Three kids lived in the fourth floor apartment; they all died. Ladder 2 was first in and did everything they could to save the kids. Bill Reese got in a third floor window and saved a little girl who was getting ready to jump. He walked a gutter with her under his arm and carried her down a ladder.

After the fire was knocked down, we were kept at the scene as one of the overhauling companies. The chief informed us that children were missing. We searched on the fourth floor and I found a girl under the chimney. She never had a chance. I guess that she heard the fire in the hallway door and opened the door. The other two were found in a closet. Children would often hide in closets to get away from the heat and smoke.

I guess the girl I found was the oldest; she was baby-sitting while the parents sat in a bar up on Cambridge Street. She was only eight...too young to die. We carried the kids out in body bags. It was tough. During the years I saw many, many deaths by fire, but youngsters always got to me.

Macarelli's was open and they made us coffee. I was sitting there, covered with debris, and I looked up. My tough blond was standing there...she put her arms around me...she was crying.

Too Late to Help

During my early years on the job, seeing death by fire was very hard for me. Of course, you never get used to it, but I think that as time went on I was able to accept it as a reality of the profession, a fact of the firefighter's life. Still, children's deaths remained very, very difficult for me throughout my career.

Shortly after I was appointed to the department we worked a three alarm fire in a tenement district of East Cambridge. It was our first alarm district, but when the box came in we were tied up at an overheated and cherry red coal furnace. The fire was in a section of Cambridge with three deckers very close to one another. A good fire in this type of building can quickly spread out the windows and ignite the curtains of the adjacent windows approximately eight feet away.

When we cleared the furnace incident we were ordered to respond to the fire. Upon arrival we were ordered to take a two and a half inch line to the roof of a garage. The wall of the garage was about five feet away from the second floor windows of the burning building. A chief officer came up the ladder and told the lieutenant to play the stream of water against the ceilings of the two rear rooms. He went on to explain that there had been a partial collapse of the second floor, and the rooms contained the dead, burnt bodies of an entire family and there was nothing we could do, they would be removing them shortly.

I had the pipe and as gently as I could I sprayed the water back and fourth across the ceiling. It was a strange feeling knowing that they were in there, as if the devastated rooms were now their tomb and we must perform our actions with reverence and respect.

As daylight came and the smoke began to clear, we could see into the rooms. Our line was then ordered to shut down. Three children, ranging in age from two to six, and one woman, the mother, had been burnt to death. As I watched them remove the blackened, stiff bodies, I remember thinking that even though they were dead there was no further damage to them after we got there. Then we were ordered off the roof.

Out on the street I sat on the rear step of the hose wagon and watched the father of the family being consoled by a Catholic priest. The father had been at work in the Woven Hose factory and had just been informed about the fire.

I still remember how I felt that morning. I still remember thinking that if only we had been able to get up on that roof a little earlier, they might not have died. If we could have even told the father that although we could not save them, at least we cooled the rooms down. If only we could have done something...more.

It had been a flash fire caused by a space heater that exploded. The mother and children never had a chance. This type of fire was common in those days. There were virtually no controls on a wick type space heater. When cold range oil (kerosene) expanded, it would flood the burner. Burning oil would now run down the side of the unit and ignite the floor. Now the burning floor would overheat the fuel tank, and an explosion followed. Flaming oil would quickly consume the entire apartment.

I remember driving home that morning and using the privacy of my car to cry. I just had to let it out. When my mother asked why my eyes were red, I said it was because of the smoke.

Ginsburg Paper Company

Even though Cambridge is a good sized city on its own and is also adjacent to the city of Boston, as late as 1951 we were still blowing factory horns for large fires. The housing project where I was living was quite close to the large and sprawling Woven Hose Factory; when there was a second alarm or greater, the fire department would notify Woven Hose and they would sound the horns on their roof. If you were off duty and heard the horns, you were supposed to report to your station. Of course, this was before overtime. We were on duty twenty-four hours a day and that was that. If you didn't like it, you were told to get another job.

The horns woke my mother at quarter past three one morning. She gave me a shake and asked me if I was supposed to go to a fire. I lay there and counted the blows. They were sounding 294 Norton Square. As far as I knew, this would be on Columbia Street somewhere.

It was a cold, damp morning and I hoped my car would start. It was a 1939 Ford and quite temperamental. After some urging and a spray of ether, the engine sprang to life. When I turned onto Cambridge Street, I could see it in the sky—dark orange clouds silhouetted against the early morning sky. The nearer I got to the fire the larger it looked.

The police had traffic stopped on Cambridge Street, so I took a short cut through the Boston & Maine Railroad freight yards As I drove through the yards I was stunned to realize that it was the Ginsburg Paper Company that was burning. The complex of two and three story buildings was located close to the city boundary between Cambridge and Somerville in the freight yard area. Both cities would eventually strike three alarms.

My company, Engine 5, would have been first-in to the fire. They had ordered a second alarm on arrival. Three of the five buildings were involved. Apparently the fire had started outside in a large paper storage yard; the wind was up and had communicated the fire to the exposed structures.

I parked my car and headed for the fire. Our pump was located at a hydrant on Columbia Street. Charlie, the pump operator, told me that the hose wagon was in the yard. Even out on the street the smoke was so thick that I had to get down on my hands and knees to follow our lines. Lieutenant Larkin and the guys were operating our deck gun. Over the roar of the fire the lieutenant told me to take his place on the gun, that he was going back to the pump. We were on the leeward side of the fire and the intense smoke and heat were right in our faces. Tod Sweeney had his helmet on backwards to break the heat waves; I followed his example and did the same.

About all we could do was to keep sweeping the deck gun back and forth in a losing attempt to keep the fire in check. The water pressure in the area was dropping seriously and arrangement for supplementary pumping would be required. This involves taking water from a distance. Pumps would lay feeder lines and connect them into pumps operating near the fire. This would improve the fire streams.

Mutual Aid companies were now arriving, and I was ordered to assist Boston Engine 22 lay feeder lines. I ended up on the top of a freight car operating a two and a half inch line with Engine 22. The cars were full of paper, but did not become involved. The first rays of the morning sun found us making little headway against the fire. After all, most of the buildings contained cardboard boxes of paper products.

Finally, at about six-thirty the fire was declared under control and mutual aid units started to make up. I gave Twenty-two a hand rolling up their line. The Salvation Army wagon was out on Columbia Street and a hot cup of coffee sure tasted good. I was scheduled to be on duty today at Engine 5. Group 7 was on duty. As I sipped my coffee I wondered if there would be time for me to go home for a while; my dungarees and shirt were soaking wet.

Lieutenant Larkin found me and told me to report to Captain Curly behind one of the storage buildings. The Rescue Company was using a winch off the front of the truck to pull smoldering bales of paper out of a freight car. Captain Curly was a big man; I knew him only by sight since he was in charge of an up-town company. He'd been acting deputy the previous night and assigned to Division 2.

It was real smoky in the car. The smell of burnt paper was extreme. We had little knowledge of the hazards of high concentrations of carbon monoxide. All I knew was that I had a hell of a headache. The cable was stretched into the car. After the hook was secured in the bale, the winch pulled it out onto the loading dock where a crew opened the bale then soaked down the paper with a one and a half inch line. This was the only way to put the damned thing out.

I didn't see Captain Curly go down. I was standing right next to him near the door when suddenly the smoke got very thick and breathing became very hard, and the captain was gone. I knelt down and could hear him coughing. He'd fallen between the loading dock and the freight car. He was dead by the time we reached him. We got him back onto the loading dock and he was transported to the Cambridge City Hospital, but there was nothing they could do for him. Later someone told me that one of the chiefs went to the rectory of Captain Curly's parish for a priest; they then went to the captain's home and broke the tragic news to his wife. We were told Captain Curly died from severe smoke inhalation. At the time the use of masks just wasn't considered very manly. I guess we were considered—and considered ourselves— "smoke eaters" and that was that. Carbon monoxide was a killer, a silent killer.

Two detail companies were left at the fire scene to complete the overhaul. I asked Lt. Larkin for permission to go and get my car. I was worried if it would start, especially when I realized that in my haste to get to the fire I had left the can of starter fluid on the street. After walking down streets and looking up alleys, it became apparent to me that I had no idea where I had parked the damned thing! Maybe it was towed away, I thought. Perhaps it was stolen. On reflection, however, grand theft auto did not seem a realistic assumption. A 1939 Ford in 1951 was not of great value on the market—legitimate or otherwise. Both rear doors were welded closed since I couldn't find hinges to fit them in Abie's junk yard. When my girl friend entered the passenger side, I would brace the door with my foot so it wouldn't fall off. In short, the car was a real bucket.

The walk back to Engine 5 was not that far. My regular crew was on duty. We loaded on dry hose and cleaned equipment. When Lieutenant Malvern asked me if I'd found my car, I told him, no, but that I hoped to have better luck after work. When a police officer came into quarters, I asked him if he could find out if the car had been towed; he returned later and said that there was no record of it.

After we got off duty that evening Billy Mac drove me down to the fire area for another look. An engine and a ladder company were still there wetting down debris. We finally found my car exactly where I had left it—behind an abandoned warehouse two blocks from the fire. I guess I hadn't paid much attention to where I was because I was so pre-occupied with where I was going!

We stood at attention outside the church for Captain Curly's funeral. I knew then that the sight of his wife and children would remain with me always—the bewildered look on her face as she clutched the hand of her young son. This boy would later become a firefighter at Ladder 3. As the years passed and I had a family of my own, whenever I left the house for work Peggy would always say, "Be careful, hon." A big hug was given to all. It could be their last.

Cast in Lead

Sunday nights are usually quiet. This one was different. About eight o'clock we received a box for a fire in the commercial district near Kendall Square. It was November and a cold, bitter wind was blowing.

The first engine arriving, Engine 7, reported heavy fire showing from a one story brick factory. The chief at the scene ordered us to take the rear and advance a big line in the rear door.

In those days only the Rescue Company wore masks on a regular basis. We hit the floor and started advancing the 2½. Unknown to us, this company manufactured lead combs and right ahead of us was a vat full of hot lead, about five hundred gallons worth. Heavy fire rolled along the ceiling. Charlie Mollar had the tip and I was backing him up. Just as Charlie opened up to hit the fire, all five hundred gallons of lead left the vat at once and Charlie was covered with burning hot lead. We both stumbled out, following the line to the door.

Charlie sat on the sidewalk, his helmet and rubber coat covered with lead. Fortunately, we both had our heads down and our faces were partially protected. He received second degree burns to the side of his face and neck. Gloves protected our hands. We both lay on the sidewalk while the guys from Engine 7 sprayed water on us. All I could think of was that Charlie looked like the Tin Man in *The Wizard of Oz*.

By the time they got us to the Mass. General, the lead had set and Charlie was about one hundred pounds heavier. They kept

Charlie, but released me. I lucked-out with second degree burns to a small section of my face and neck. Charlie spent a week in the hospital while they picked lead out of his moustache! Finally they gave up and shaved it off. I think this hurt Charlie more than the lead.

On Duty?

Sometimes the old fire station could be a home away from home. I remember one lieutenant attached to Engine 5 who was going through a divorce and was sleeping-in when he was off duty. I asked him one day how he knew whether he was on or off duty when an alarm came in at night. He told me that when the lights went on he would look for his night hitch; if it was by his bed, he would get up and respond; if it wasn't, back to sleep he'd go.

One night he returned to the station from the Orange Club where he'd done a little dancing. After he retired, I put his hitch by his bed and sure enough an alarm hit for a building fire about three in the morning. Up he jumped, saw the night hitch and down the pole he slid. He tried to get on the rig, but the on-duty officer told him to go back upstairs and back to bed.

Naturally I denied any responsibility.

I pulled this stunt a few times. One night, when I thought he was asleep, I moved the night hitch from the closet to beside his bed. He sat up and in a deep, authoritative voice said, "Take your hands off that, you little Irish bastard!"

I never pulled that one again.

After-Shave

Over a cup of coffee one morning, Ron reported to the captain that someone was stealing his after-shave lotion. Engine 5 had a number of small rooms on the second floor that were used as bunk rooms. Usually two men were assigned to each. Ron told the captain that he strongly suspected him roommate. After all, they worked in different groups and were never there at the same time. The captain suggested to Ron that he had more important matters on his mind than possibly stolen after-shave and to solve the problem himself.

About a month later we were sitting in the kitchen in the morning, drinking our coffee, and the captain asked Ron how he'd made out with the problem of the missing lotion.

"Well, Captain, now that you ask," Ron responded, "I did solve it myself. You see, I took the cap off and pissed in the bottle until it was full. You know, Cap, the damnedest part of it is that now *the bottle is half empty!* I tell ya, some guys'll use anything."

The captain just shook his head.

Christine

She was stunning. Blond hair, blue eyes, about 120 pounds. I first saw her at Stanley's house during a party. She was his cousin, Christine, from Springfield. Stanley was a spark who hung around our firehouse and even rode with us from time to time. When I asked him about this girl, he said that she was eighteen and a very talented musician.

She was perfect for me. After all, I was twenty-two! One night Stanely was at the station and I asked him to fix me up with this girl. I had already made up my mind that I was going to marry her. He told me that she'd won a scholarship to the New England Conservatory of Music and would be studying piano. He also told me she would be staying at his house while she was going go school.

I had an old Ford coupe at the time and offered to Pick Christine up with Stan at the North Station when she arrived from Springfield. On the way to the train station I asked him for some special greeting I could give her in Polish. He replied, "Say *padupa spelzee*. This is a very old, very flattering saying for a lady."

I said the words over and over to get my special greeting just right and Stan would correct my pronunciation. When he was satisfied with what he heard, he added, "Don't forget to bow deep when you say it because it makes it more effective. It's really a nice touch."

There we stood. She had just stepped off the train. She was

beautiful. I bowed deep and, in my very best voice, said, "Christine...*padupa spelzee.*" She immediately hit me over the head with her pocketbook and started to yell at me while Stan doubled over with laughter. I had just told the girl of my dreams, my lady love that her bottom smelled bad—in Polish.

Christine never spoke to me again, even though Stan's mother explained the situation to her. I think Stan's mother hit him over the head a few times too.

The Writing on the Wall

Since I was only twenty-two and dating girls, I was broke most of the time. Charlie Mollar lent me money and kept a record of the debt that I and others owed him. He used the wall behind his bed for a financial ledger and wrote all the debts there. One day the captain assigned us to wash the walls, so I grabbed my bucket and sponge and raced for the wall behind Charlie's bed. I was busy rubbing out all debts when I heard a loud yell coming from the area where Charlie was working, then I heard someone running down the hall towards Charlie's room. "You bastard, O'Brien!" Charlie bellowed. "Did you rub out my record? It's the only one I got." He looked at the clean wall behind his bed and started to whimper.

Handing him a piece of paper, I assured him that I had made a true copy of his ledger before I started to wash.

"Twenty! Twenty bucks! That's all?" he cried.

"Ya, Charlie," I affirmed. "You know I wouldn't cheat you."

Some years later Charlie and I were talking over old times, and when the wall washing incident came up I pulled a twenty dollar bill from my wallet and handed it to him. Charlie took it and said, "There'll be three dollars more in interest."

Charlie did keep a close eye on his wallet. He didn't waste a dollar. For example, when he needed a new set of false teeth, rather than taking them back to the doctor for adjustment, he would grind them down on the wheel in the shop. He was also a fanatic about the condition of his car. If he heard a squeak, he would spend hours trying to find it. When he located the source of the annoying noise, he'd stick pieces of an old inner tube between the metal parts. When he'd go upstairs I'd sneak into the garage and remove the tubes. He'd drive home the next day with the same squeak or rattle driving him crazy.

One day the lieutenant was leaning over the apparatus door watching Charlie sweep the ramp. I was washing the hose wagon. The lieutenant called me over to the half door and said, "Look, Obie." When I looked where pointed there was a twenty dollar bill laying on the ground. Oh boy, I thought.

Over the door I leaped, but alas...too late. My good friend Charlie had leaned over and picked up the twenty.

"What a damned shame, Obie," the lieutenant said. "You could have used that money on your date tonight."

Later in the day I was forced to visit the loan office in Charlie's room. Sometime later I learned that Charlie knew my financial situation and had thrown the twenty onto the ramp. I also discovered that the lieutenant was in on the charade.

Charlie once sold me a rock maple kitchen set, and in our spare time we refinished it using a special varnish stain. Our efforts resulted in some very beautiful furniture. I left it set up in the rear garage to dry real well. Then one of the boys decided to use my beautiful table as an ironing board; when they got a call for a bedroom fire, he forgot to pull the plug on the iron. That was the end of my table.

Charlie was retiring due to health reasons when I was promoted to lieutenant. The guys threw a grand bash for me and Charlie on the third floor over the station. The beer, however, was kept cold in the officers' bath tub on the second floor. There was a set of circular metal stairs from the third floor to the second floor window; these stairs got quite a workout that night. In those days it was customary for the working group to attend such a time, but I can honestly say that I never saw an on-duty fireman unfit for duty. It was a part of the unwritten code of conduct.

The lieutenant working that night, Harry Magoon, came up to the third floor at ten-thirty and told us to take the party in town—the neighbors were beginning to complain. Harry was winding his alarm clock as if to make his point absolutely clear.

The boys said that if they had to leave they were taking the bath tub with them. One jake produced a wrench and started to disconnect the tub. Cooler head prevailed and the party went across the square to the establishment we called "The Bucket of Blood Pub."

Charlie was placed over someone's shoulder and carried across the street, a ride he enjoyed immensely. Top Shelf Sullivan, the bartender at the Bucket of Blood, set up the bar. I was due at my new assignment at 7:00 a.m. the next morning, so needless to say I was not too well off. The captain of Engine 9 took me on a tour of a new hospital facility. A kind nurse saw my poor face and pulled me into a room where she gave me a few shots of oxygen. Somehow I survived the day.

The police closed the Bucket of Blood at four in the morning. Top Shelf was a non-drinker, so everyone arrived home OK. Everyone, that is, except Charlie.

Charlie Mollar had fallen asleep in a booth at the Bucket. Top Shelf Sullivan didn't notice Charlie curled up in his impromptu bunk as he was closing up and locked Charlie inside. When the bar's owner found Charlie the next, Charlie suggested they send out for some food and continue the party. The owner called Charlie a cab.

We mailed the bar bill to Charlie, but he'd already left town for Florida.

Carstine's Coal Yard

Another Easter Sunday...working. Easter was getting to be quite an event for the Cambridge Fire Department. In the early sixties, we had a series of multiple alarm fires that occurred on East Sunday. None of these jobs were connected in any way; they just happened, and they happened in various parts of the city on Easter Sunday. Maybe it was due to some kind of cycle were in. After a few years on the job, I believed in cycles; that if, for example, you had two runs it was almost certain that there was a third out there waiting for you. Fires seemed to come in bunches. I began to hate it when things became too quiet because I knew a big job was coming.

There would be no dinner in the station on this Easter Sunday. Most of the guys had made arrangements for a man for man relief. As soon as your man came in you could leave. This was done with the house captain's approval and only on holidays; sometimes for a special event, like the firefighters' ball, an order with approval would come down from headquarters. Easter was always a special day. There was a church down the street, and it was almost a neighborhood ritual for the kids, all dressed up in their spiffy new Easter clothes, to stop by the fire station on their way back from church; we would stand at the apparatus half door and tell them all how great they looked.

Carstine's Coal Yard was located in North Cambridge. The area around it was a combination of factories and three decker, multiple occupancy dwellings. The Boston and Maine Railroad tracks ran along the rear of the property, and three or four very large wood sheds used for the storage of coal were located along the railroad tracks. Coal-carrying gondolas were at a rear siding waiting to be unloaded. A large one story garage where the delivery trucks were kept was also part of the complex. Carstine's was a busy operation that employed over twenty people. After all, at this time most people still used coal in their central heating systems, and in some cases even in the kitchen stove.

Box 7851 hit at 10:45 a.m. on April 15, 1962. The weather was warm and dry; the wind was out of the southwest, and we had not seen any rain for quite awhile. I had just come downstairs and was sitting at the patrol desk. Billy McCall had just finished refueling the pump and hose wagon. He was complaining that the members of Group Five were the only ones to put gas into the apparatus. All the morning reports were on the desk waiting for the deputy to pick them up. When I looked up I saw his car pull up on the apron. Suddenly his driver put the dome lights on and away they sped. I also saw people pointing and looking up Beacon Street. Billy opened the half apparatus door, took a look and came running back in. His face was dead serious as he said, "Jesus Christ, Obie! The sky's black." Just then I heard Fire Alarm calling C3 and telling them that they were receiving calls for a fire in the freight shed at Carstine's Coal Yard. Engine 4, which is quartered about four blocks from the yard, was yelling, "On the orders of Lieutenant Splaine, strike the second alarm on box 7851."

Engine 4 had just cleared the apron of the ramp when the lieutenant ordered that a third alarm be transmitted. They had not yet turned up Massachusetts Ave. when Fire Alarm acknowledged their orders.

Now the remainder of our crew was sliding the pole and hitting the floor. The city gongs above the patrol desk were striking the box number. We were scheduled on the assignment card to respond on the second alarm. Engines were starting as the lieutenant opened the apparatus doors. I was riding the rear step that day, and I was pulling on my rubber coat as we turned left to proceed up Beacon Street toward North Cambridge.

The sight ahead of me was one that I will never forget. The sky was a deep jet black over a mile wide and framed in brilliant blue. A sense of dread came over me and made me shudder and for a moment I truly felt fear. Billy had the Federal siren opened at its highest pitch.

When we reached Porter Square, flames were visible above the tree line. The wind was blowing briskly from the southwest and large chunks of burning embers were being carried skyward. The pump stopped briefly at Walden and Mass Ave. and some chief gave the lieutenant directions for approach. At the corner of Walden and Richdale Avenue, Leo, the pump operator, found a good hydrant. Water in this area was not a problem; a thirty-six inch water main with twelve inch branches runs down Mass. Ave. We dropped two 2½" lines from the hose wagon. The lieutenant jumped on the back step and we played the line down Richdale Ave. We had passed over the railroad tracks on Walden Street and were now parallel with the fire, separated from it by the tracks. We were also on the windward side. The sight in front of us was truly awesome. Fire was absolutely everywhere. All the sheds were heavily involved and the fire was spreading. Some of the trucks parked in the garage were full of heating oil. The thermal column was rising rapidly hundreds of feet in the air. The buildings on our right shielded us from the heat as we passed them. Where there was an opening, the blast of heat almost took our breaths away. Radiant heat will travel 360 degrees in all directions, even against the wind. This fire looked like it had conflagration possibilities.

The wagon stopped where we were shielded from the heat and we pulled off extra hose. I held the male end while Billy screwed on the play pipe. My hand was shaking and Billy had difficulty making the connection. "For the love of Christ, Obie, will you hold the damn thing steady!" I think his hand was shaking a bit too. A chief I did not recognize met us and told the lieutenant to take the line in between the houses—the fire was crossing the tracks due to radiant heat.

Lt. Mullen ran ahead between the houses. He never saw the clothes line; it caught him right across the throat. I happened to look up and saw it in time. The lieutenant was outlined by flame

—38—

and did a spin backwards. He landed on his back and lay stunned. We advanced the line up to the lieutenant. He was groggy and sitting up. The heat was very, very intense. I had never seen, had never felt anything like it.

The line was now charged and we had water. Billy and I kept the nozzle closed and assisted the lieutenant out to the street where medical personnel took charge of him. Following the line back to the pipe was like crawling into a blast furnace. We opened the nozzle and held it over our heads. Some kind of small shed was ahead of us and we maneuvered the line behind it to break up the heat waves. From this angle it was difficult to play water on the exposed wooden dwellings due to the pressure on the line. Now the paint was melting and the wood was smoking. The exposed parts of our faces and hands were burning. Billy and I both turned our helmets around backward to break the heat that was burning our faces. It was getting hard to breathe. The rumble of flame across the tracks was now a loud roar.

We swept the line back and forth, back and forth, hitting the eaves section of the roofs, letting the water cascade down. We were trying to cool down the exposed dwellings and keep the fire from jumping the tracks. The only problem was that the water was turning to steam and the steam was doing little good. The heat now had us pinned down and backing out was impossible. With our backs to the tracks, we held the line over our heads and tried to get as close to the ground as possible. My rubber coat was starting to smoke.

Billy turned the pattern to a fog stream and we held it over our heads. I remember wishing that I could dig a hole in the dirt to get away from the heat. The shed we were using for a heat barrier was now on fire and globs of hot tar were falling on our coats and down our necks.

Another charged line was advancing between the building and toward us. They held their stream on us and things started to improve. The fire was now a general alarm and help was getting into operation. Other crews were moving in on the main body of the fire. The sheds across the tracks were now nothing more than shells and were starting to collapse. This type of fire will hit what is called a crown situation. When most of the fuel is burnt, it will suddenly subside. Prior to that happening, however, there is a rush of air toward the flame. This is fresh oxygen rushing in to replace that which the fire has already consumed. The rate of the rise of super-heated air is in direct proportion to the intensity of the fire. I have seen people's hats fly off and sail toward a large volume of flame.

Fresh crews were now relieving those working at the fire scene. Boston Engine 22 took our line and we headed out to Richdale Avenue for a smoke and a drink of water. Today the dangers of dehydration are better understood; we were "just thirsty." Today's firefighter is treated at a "rehab station"; we didn't fully know the danger we were in.

Billy and I were sitting on the rear step of our hose wagon when I spotted Jimmy Harrington. He was riding in the front seat of Boston Ladder 15. He had third degree burns to both ears and blood was running down his face. The lieutenant said that they were on their way back to a cover assignment and would drop him off at the hospital. Jimmy was assigned to Engine 9 and they had located in an open area down from us. Their position soon became untenable and they were forced to abandon the wagon and run for their lives. At the time there were three 2½" lines running into the deck gun mounted on the rear of the piece. "Bousser" Cook broke his ankle jumping off the deck. We later noted that the front of the hose wagon was burnt black and the windshield was destroyed. On the other side of the tracks the boys had their hands full. Four buildings were demolished or badly damaged before they could stop the spread of the fire.

When we asked about our lieutenant's condition, we were told that he had been transported to Cambridge Hospital. We learned later that he had sustained a deep bruise to his neck in the vicinity of his Adam's apple and would be off duty for a bit of time. He was always quite a singer, but some say that after tangling with the clothes line, he had dropped two registers and was even better.

The night crew was now arriving and we would be relieved at the fire scene. This was always a great deal because the tasks of rolling hose and finding missing equipment fell on the night crew. Our hose wagon was stripped. We lost two plaster hooks, two playpipes, a burst hose jacket, and seven length of two and a half inch hose. Also a partridge in a pear tree. Other companies had borrowed this equipment; it could have been anywhere. On the day after a fire like this one, a service truck would pick up extra equipment and take it to headquarters. If you were missing anything you could go up there and check the pile on the floor.

When we returned to our own quarters, I took a shower. The cold water sure felt good. When I looked in the mirror I saw that my face and neck were a nice red color. If anyone asked about my face, I told them I'd spent the day in the sun.

The Polish Flag

On New Year's Eve we responded to a second alarm fire in the Polish Club on Main Street. The club had had a party earlier in the evening, but everyone had gone home by the time the alarm came in, which was a good thing because when we arrived on the scene the fire was really going good with very heavy smoke and fire in the rear. We advanced a two and a half inch line in the rear door and started knocking down the fire as we went. The smoke was down to the floor. As I crawled along I felt a leg and realized someone was standing near the bar. It was a Cambridge cop.

When they got him outside, they asked him what the hell he was doing in there. He replied that his sergeant told him to prevent the fireman from stealing the booze! He had taken quite a bit of smoke but was otherwise OK.

When the fire was knocked down we started overhauling the area, checking for extension and killing hot spots. Now at this time, television was a very new development; not everyone had one or two or three at home. The Polish Club had a set mounted on the balcony railing where the patrons could watch it from the bar below. Bill and I tried to hook the TV and save it, but it got away from us and smashed to the floor. Oh well, we tried.

I noticed a Polish flag hanging behind the bar; I took it down and folded it before it could be ruined. I placed the flag in a cabinet drawer behind the bar for safe keeping.

About eight months later the club reopened. My pal, John, and I suspected a good supply of attractive women would be at the club for the re-opening, so we decided to investigate. Being

Irish and not Polish, however, did present a problem. A big bouncer greeted us at the front door with a hearty "Members only!" I looked at him for a bit and then asked, "If I can tell you where you guys found the club's Polish flag after the fire, will you let us in?" He not only let us in, but I was made a card carrying honorary member of the Cambridge Polish Club. Our money was no good and we had a hell of a party.

Fortunately, they never found out that I was also responsible for the smashed television.

A Fine Battery

When we got to the car parked behind the barroom located next to our firehouse, it was pretty well involved. We knocked the fire down quickly and started to overhaul.

A full box alarm had been sounded for the incident because fire was visible from the street and Fire Alarm was receiving calls. The chief was there, and as part of the procedure we popped the hood and...lo and behold—no battery. Someone wondered aloud how a car without a battery ended up behind the pub.

We were getting a rash of stolen car fires in the area. Kids would steal the car and after they were finished with their joyride or their business, they torched it. Just then a boy about nine years old said to the chief, "Hey, Mister, you looking for the battery?"

The Cambridge police officer who had respond on the alarm of fire said, "Yeah, as a matter of fact we are. Waddaya know?"

"Guy in the bar's got it," said the boy and he was gone.

In the back door of the pub we go and sitting there all by himself was this young guy with the map of Ireland on his face and a beer in front of him. The cop asked him if he owned the car. He replied that yes, the car was his. The cop then asked where the battery was. The fellow responded that it was right there on the floor beside him. He is now asked if he set the fire. He replied, "Yes, yes I did, but it seemed a shame to burn a perfectly fine battery, so sure I decided to save it."

We all just shook our heads as the police officer told him to drink up, that they had an appointment to keep.

Keeping the Heat Up

One of my duties as a rookie was to keep the heat up in the station. During the winter a massive coal fired furnace in the cellar supplied the heat. There was a small side-arm heater next to it that heated the water in the summertime. The big furnace was a real dog. On damp days it would go out no matter what you did. It was impossible to shake it down because the grates were very old and were held up by bricks. When I came on duty in the morning, the first thing I would do was to go down to the basement and shake the grates very gently, then shovel a few scoops of coal on. A few times I forgot and tried to poke it into life and was greeted by a massive sheet of flame out the door, which always blew the doors off. It was not my favorite rookie chore.

We finally had a new guy assigned to the company and the furnace automatically became his responsibility. Over a cup of coffee one morning, I warned Tommy of the cantankerous devil in the cellar. Tommy was a bit of a smart-ass and wouldn't listen to my voice of experience.

Later in the day I was sitting at the patrol desk when Tommy descended to the depths to poke the furnace into new life. Suddenly, an explosion nearly lifted the floor and black smoke poured up the stairs, followed by Tommy still carrying the poker. His clothes were as black as the soot that hit him.

A box was struck for a fire in the firehouse and confusion reigned for a while. Tommy was not hurt, but he did learn a hard lesson.

Some years later the city finally got around to replacing the coal furnace with oil. The problem with oil was that it had no character. The old coal furnace was like a sleeping dragon. I would sneak up on it and with my trusty lance I would poke it into new life. Occasionally it would fling open its mouth and expose the slumbering flames within. It would then shudder and accept a few shovels of coal. Oil just doesn't have the heart of a dragon.

Angel's Gloves

One night during a particularly cold and snowy winter we had a four alarm fire in a furniture warehouse. It was about three a.m. when we were ordered to return to our own quarters. We were all frozen. the hose lines were like iron pipes. The booster line was frozen solid and we wrapped it around the radiator to thaw. The lieutenant told one man at a time to go upstairs and change to dry clothes; the rest of us started packing dry hose and checking equipment. We were in quarters about ten minutes when the phone started ringing. It was Fire Alarm ordering us to respond to a building fire on Portland Street. Orders are orders, so we piled as much dry hose as we could onto the wagon and off we went.

Snow was still falling and the temperature was about ten degrees above zero. We were first due in and as we turned onto Portland Street from Cambridge Street heavy fire as showing from a row of tenements. The pump operator applied the brakes and started to skid in a circle. I was riding the rear step of the hose wagon and when our driver hit the brakes we also joined the circle. The hose in the bed was pushing on my chest while I tried to crawl up on top of the wagon to avoid being crushed. We finally stopped spinning and realized that for some strange reason we did not collide.

The fire was another cold one and all the crew, including the lieutenant, went to the hospital for frostbite. I was the only one left; an officer at the scene told me to run the pump. The fire went to three alarms and we were eventually relieved at the scene. Just after daybreak we were told to start making up. Before starting to roll hose, I stopped to light a cigarette; I put my work gloves on the fender of the truck. Naturally when I went to put my gloves back on they were frozen sold; I couldn't get my fingertips in.

We usually carried a few pairs of old gloves stuffed behind the gas tank. Unfortunately, with two large fires during the same night, someone had already used the spare gloves. God, my hands were cold! There wasn't a soul around—and then I saw him. He was standing on the sidewalk across the street from where the pump was hooked up. He was looking at me and I looked back. He smiled and motioned for me to come over. As I approached him he held out a pair of black fur-lined gloves to me.

I took the gloves and put them on. God, they were nice and warm! The man may have been on his way to work, I don't know. All I do know is that I thanked him and I do remember his smile. Needless to say, the gloves were ruined in the process of rolling frozen or soaked hose.

I bought a new pair of black fur-lined gloves to replace the pair I had ruined, and for a long time I kept an eye out for my generous benefactor, but I never saw him again. I will always remember his face, but I have a feeling that when I do see him again the gloves will not be too important.

Dump Duty

Back in the fifties we had a very large municipal dump located in North Cambridge. It burned twenty-four hours a day. When you reported for work, the first thing you did was to check the blackboard to see who was up for the dump. If it was going pretty well or if there was too much smoke in the neighborhood, Fire Alarm would start getting calls and the Division 2 deputy would go up and take a look. If you were the next due engine to go, the Fire Alarm operator would call and tell you to dress warm or to bring your lunch.

Dump duty was very dirty work. During the summer it was hot and smokey. During the winter you froze, really froze. All you could really do was knock down the surface fire with a deck gun and then break down to two and a half inch hand lines and bury the tip in the rubbish. After that it was just a matter of holding the hose there and flooding it out.

One really cold night Bill McCall and I were both kneeling down, working a hose. The smoke was extemely heavy; visibility was nearly zero. Something smelled truly awful—even for the dump!—and when I asked Bill if he ever took a bath, he said he was about to ask me the same question!

We were on that line most of the night and when it started to get light we found the source of the smell. We had been sitting on top of a dead dog throughout the entire night. The dog never complained, but we sure did.

Another night Lieutenant Cooper was off by himself, scouring the dump, looking for a hinge to replace a broken one on the refrigerator door at the station. Bill and I were working a line on a steep bank when off in the distance through the smoke I saw a light suddenly drop and go out. It didn't look right, so I mentioned it to Bill. On a hunch we shut down the line and went to investigate. As we approached the spot, we could hear Lt. Cooper yelling for help.

The "ground" was all layers of rubbish, perhaps fifty feet deep, and the fire was burning underground. The lieutenant had fallen through the surface up to his elbows and into a hole with roaring fire beneath him. We got as close as we could, then lay on the rubbish and threw him a hose rope. We were able to get the lieutenant out, but it was very, very close.

Another day when we were operating at the dump, a man came running up and told us that when he moved old furniture out of his late mother's house it was all tossed in the dump. His brother had called him and told that his mom—who did not trust banks—had stashed a large sum of money taped under a bureau drawer. We asked when the furniture had been dumped and he said just that morning.

The problem was that the area of the morning dumping was going like hell. We shagged our line over there and went to work on the fire. When it was safe for him to search for his estate, we gave him a hand. After about an hour of searching, he found his mother's bureau. He pulled open the drawers and found his fortune—twenty-five one dollar bills!

We spent a few Christmases and New Year's Eves at the dump, singing carols or wishing each other a great new year. The fires below didn't know they were going on a holiday.

One officer on Engine 8 had a reputation for being a tinkerer, the kind of fellow who could fix anything from a broken clock to a hi-fi system. On this particular night both Engines 8 and 9 were at the dump. I was a lieutenant on Nine. Engine 8 was working on our right flank. I could see the tinkering lieutenant working half way down the bank. I thought this was strange, so I took a walk over there. Apparently, a large department store had hired a salvage company to haul away tools that had been discontinued. They were just thrown in the dump, about one hundred cases of them. Dirt had been piled on top, but the hose streams had washed it away, revealing a bonanza for any tinkerer. The lieutenant and his crew were salvaging tools of every description. Some had a handle broken or some other small defect, but all worth saving. Our hose wagon made a few trips back to the station that night; and you could safely assume that we all became owners of full sets of slightly bruised tools.

When the captain came on duty in the morning, he took one look at the tools laid out on the floor and asked what the hell was going on. I informed him of our good fortune and told him there was a tool box for him. I only heard a grunt and orders to clean up the mess.

The captain was seen later in the day placing his new tools in the trunk of his car.

Many Red Faces

Fires in hospitals are very rare primarily because they have rigorous maintenance and housekeeping programs and strict patient supervision. This particular call was not for a fire in the hospital but in the nursing students' residence.

For the Cambridge Fire Department, a hospital box generally requires three engine companies, two ladder companies, a rescue unit and a chief. Engine 5 was located about five blocks away from Mercy Hospital, so we were in there first. Smoke was showing from the cellar windows of a two and a half story wood frame dwelling detached from the main hospital. Lieutenant Cooper ordered a big line laid to the front of the building.

I was driving the hose wagon that day. For training purposes we alternated drivers on both pieces. The big line was reduced to a one and a half inch hose and taken in the front door. As I advanced the tip, I could see heavy smoke coming up the cellar stairs. Everything indicated that we had a cellar fire.

The lieutenant and Don McNair were behind me as I descended the stairs. The ladder guys were busy opening up in order to allow the smoke to escape. Rescue was searching to make sure everyone got out. Fortunately, the fire came in near dinner time, so most of the nursing students were over at the hospital.

The problem was that I could not find *any fire* to extinguish. In those days we did not wear masks, and this smoke could really cut your heart out. We searched and searched until we finally found the source of the smoke—a large, disconnected hot air furnace.

Inside the furnace we found a good sized pile of smoldering rags and very little fire. I pulled them out with my gloved hand and they were extinguished. All the hot air pipes leading from the boiler were down on the floor, thus the smoke condition.

Lieutenant Cooper said it seemed a little suspicious and notified the deputy to come down to the cellar. We were all staring at the pile of rags, trying to figure what had happened when Don said, "Unless I miss my guess, boys, we are looking at a pile of sanitary napkins." Closer examination proved Donny was correct. When the deputy notified the head nursing instructor of our discovery, she was furious. She called every nursing student living in the residence to the basement, and with stern admonition, she demanded that the culprits admit to the act.

By this time we were all bailing out of the cellar. There the young girls stood, crying, mortified, while madam read them the riot act. One by one we climbed the stairs; only the deputy remained to witness the students' embarrassment. Later he said it was one of the more difficult situations he'd had to endure.

The Dewey and Almy Fire

Barbara and Al had never met Peggy. I'd told them about her and how sure I was that she was the one for me. We had plans for Saturday night: I would pick up Peg at her home in South Boston and then we'd have dinner with Al and Barbara at their house. I'd known Al all my life; we grew up together in North Cambridge. I was his best man when he and Barbara married.

Peggy and I chatted a bit excitedly about our life together as I drove across the Mass. Ave. Bridge. There was no indication that this would be a night to remember.

Ladder 3 and Engine 2 are located on Mass. Ave. near the bridge. Jug Daily was standing in front of the station, and when he saw me he started to wave furiously. I pulled over and he hurried across the street with an excited look on his face. "Connie, they just struck the second alarm for Dewey and Almy on Whittemore Ave. They're talking about a chemical fire."

In those days you were required to report to your station on the second alarm and stand by for orders. Overtime pay was unheard of. You were a firefighter twenty-four hours a day, and if you didn't like it—get another job.

When we got to Inman Square, Engine 5 had already responded on the second alarm. The procedure detailed that a firefighter should report to the company at the fire. I grabbed my helmet, rubber coat, boots and a spanner belt and headed for the fire. "Don't worry, Peg," I said, "this won't take long. I'll just report to the company, explain I've got a date and we'll be over Al's house in an hour."

Peg looked at me with that knowing glance, as much as to say, "That's not how it's going to go, Connie." She was right. Once we parted I didn't see her for three days.

By the time we reached the fire, it was already three alarms. Dewey and Almy was a large manufacturing complex that covered four square blocks. It housed offices, research facilities, chemical storage and manufacturing plants. They had recently received a very large and lucrative contract to manufacture large neoprene observation balloons for the government. These balloons were forty feet in circumference and stored in underground vaults where they hung perpendicular to dry. At the time of the fire, fifty or so of the balloons were in storage.

I found a place to park on Seagrave Road, gave Peggy a hurried kiss and headed for the fire.

The involved building was a two story, second class (wood and brick) with a flat roof. There was no visible fire, only heavy brown-yellow colored smoke. Lieutenant Malvern called me over to the hose wagon: "Connie, we're going to take in a two and a half." We entered the building through a loading platform door. Pinky Welsh was on the pipe, the lieutenant was behind him, and I was backing up the line supporting it as they moved forward. We were wearing "all-service" type masks which could protect you down to 16% oxygen and 2% poison gas.

Visibility in the building was zero. I could hear a sprinkler working somewhere ahead of us. We crawled over some kind of conveyer racks. Later I found out that it was the pit area where the balloons were stored to dry! There was no fire to hit, only mercilessly heavy smoke. We moved the line deeper into the building. Then I heard a muffled voice ahead almost yelling, "Back out! Back out!" Then I could see it, and I ducked as the rolling orange flame shot over our heads and the intense heat pushed us down to the floor. The explosion passed over our heads; our line was now operating, and scalding hot water poured down my neck.

Again the urgent voice: "For Christ's sake, back out!" The line was thrashing now and I moved forward toward the pipe. Both Pinky and the lieutenant were gone. With my gloved hand I tried to control the nozzle and shut down the line. To leave the hose would mean death; the hose would show me the way out.

The strong taste of rubber smoke began seeping through my mask. The canister of the mask was red hot and getting ready to quit. "Pinky! Lute!" I yelled, but there was no answer to my call. Keeping the hose between my knees, backward I crawled. The hose was sagging in front me; it had been pulled across a pit.

I heard voices now to my left. Another company was advancing a line in. I could see a belt light. They've found me, I thought to myself, thank God they've found me. Once we'd reached the outside, they asked me where the other men were. The Rescue Company followed the line into where we were operating, but they couldn't go too far because the area was full of pits.

The fire was getting worse. Great billows of acrid smoke were pumping from the building. We'd gone into outside operations and men began dropping like flies. When the wind direction changed, the Rescue made another effort to enter the building from the windward side. Just inside the door of the loading dock, they found the rest of my crew. Both Pinky and Lieutenant Malvern were in really bad shape. Neither one ever returned to duty.

A total of seventy-eight firefighters were taken to area hospitals, most for smoke inhalation. They said that the corridors of Cambridge City Hospital looked like a war zone. Peggy told me later that she looked into each ambulance that left the scene. No one could give her any information about me. She never forgot that night. It's no wonder she felt the way she did about me being a firefighter. I never fully realized her anguish. I could try, but I could never succeed. None of us can. None of us can know fully the anguish, the fear, our profession bestows on those we love. Every loved one, woman or man, who sits and waits for the phone to ring is truly a special person.

Memorial Hall

Deputy Chief O'Connell had a department wide reputation as a great kidder. I remember one night I was sitting at the desk doing floor patrol when he came into quarters. He congratulated me on my recent marriage to Peggy. I thanked him and then he asked if Peggy minded being alone nights when I was on duty. I replied that it was part of the job. He now looked at his driver and said, "Poor Peggy, she's all alone at home! She must be lonely, Connie. Are *you* lonely, Connie?"

"No, sir, I'm fine, sir," I told him.

He seemed on a roll and continued speaking to his aide: "You know, Al, poor Connie is lonely for his new bride. I wonder if we can do anything about this?" He then walked over to the pole hole and yelled up, "Lieutenant Malvern, I'm sending Firefighter O'Brien home so he can cuddle with his wife."

At that time, 1954, Peggy and I had a third floor apartment on Inman Street just around the corner from the firehouse. She was ironing when I walked into the apartment. "Hi, hon! How come you're home?" I told her that the chief had sent me home to hug her. "That was nice of him, hon," she said, "but I have ironing to do." We were having a cup of coffee in our little kitchen when I heard the outside siren going off up at the firehouse. "Hon, I think you just missed a run," Peggy said. I turned on my old tank radio set BC 683 just in time to hear Lieutenant Malvern order a working fire in a block of stores on Cambridge Street.

When I walked into the station, a covering engine company

was just backing in. I told them that I had been sent on an errand for the deputy and had just returned. When Deputy O'Connell called for another engine company, I responded with the covering company. It turned out to be a shed fire in the rear of a Chinese restaurant that had extended into the main building. I guess it was quite smokey for a while, and they had to do a good deal of pulling metal ceilings. I reported to Lieutenant Malvern and went to work. Neither he nor the deputy ever mentioned my absence.

Several years later, Chief O'Connell stopped in at Engine 5 one afternoon to make a phone call; I again had floor patrol and was sitting at the desk. He was talking casually with someone on the phone when he shifted the conversation to another individual; his tone became more agitated, then he suddenly hung up, looked at me and said, "Obie, Memorial Hall is on fire! That was Fire Alarm—they're striking a box." By this time I had learned that the chief was a kidder, so I didn't take his announcement too seriously. He and his aide took off in the red car, sirens and lights going. "Nice touch!" I said to no one in particular.

Just then the bells started ringing and off we went. I was riding the rear step of the hose wagon, and as we started up Cambridge Street, I could see heavy smoke showing from the bell-clock tower of Memorial Hall. Bill McCall was in the open front seat and he was yelling at me and pointing to the smoke.

Memorial Hall is a Harvard University building. It was built shortly after to Civil War to commemorate the Harvard students and graduates who were killed during the war. Memorial Hall is an enormous building of wood and brick construction covering about two city blocks. When people see Memorial Hall for the first time, they often think it's a church. In recent years Harvard used the building for various purposes; it also housed Sanders Theatre, the university radio station, library rooms and many priceless paintings.

Memorial Hall had a partial sprinkler system at this time that covered mainly the theatre and basement rooms. Workmen had been re-flashing the clock tower and using open flame. When we arrived on the scene, fire was showing from the top and sides of the bell tower. Chief Larkin met us and ordered us to assist Ladder 1 in throwing a forty-five foot ladder to the front side of the building on Broadway. As we were removing the ladder from the truck, I saw the left rear tiller wheel lift. The stick was fully extended and Lt. Tim O'Connell was attaching the ladder pipe. The truck was up on the lawn and the ground was not firm. We tried to push the ladder back, but it was too late. The stick fell against the side of the building. Lt. O'Connell was knocked off the ladder and was hanging by one hand forty feet above the street.

Somehow the lieutenant was able to hold on and get back on the aerial. The forty-five was thrown and the poles set. The tip of the fully extended ladder still did not reach the round window. The clock tower is about 175 feet high.

We were now ordered to take the 150 foot hauling line and make our way to the room with the round window. A custodian volunteered to show us the way. When we reached the balcony over the main hall I noticed there was a pale of smoke at the ceiling level of the auditorium. The custodian showed us the door to the stairs that led to the clock tower, then Lt. Cooper thanked him and told him that was far enough for him, that we'd find our way up to the room.

The wainscot covered stairway twisted and turned, eventually leading to a room approximately twenty feet by twenty feet. To the left a door led to a catwalk over the interior of the rotunda. Three members of the Rescue Company were crossing the catwalk towards us. They had climbed a circular metal fire escape on the Oxford Street side of the building. Their mission was the same as ours—get a hose through the window and operate on the fire.

We opened the window and realized the tip of the forty-five foot ladder was at least fifty feet below us. There was a guy with a two and a half inch play pipe on his shoulder yelling for the hauling line. We pulled the hose up and into the room. There was no direct way to get to the clock tower from that room, so we operated the hose to cool the ceiling and kill flaming embers that were falling down the vent shaft.

Just then we lost water. The high pressure required to lift water so high had backed the hose right out of the coupling. The hose was replaced and again we hit the ceiling. Again we lost water—a burst hose. As we waited for the line to be replaced, Lt. Cooper told me to check the stairs that we'd used to come up since the smoke was really starting to bank down.

I made my way to the door of the stairs. The smoke was so thick that I could hardly see the rays of my belt light. As I backed down the stairs I could feel the heat coming up. When I reached the balcony I could hear men below me yelling that the fire was below and spreading upward. When I got back to the room where we were working, Lt. Cooper was not happy with my report. They were still playing water on the ceiling. Just then "the lights went out"—the smoke dropped to floor and we started to suffocate. The Rescue had all-service masks; we had none.

We took turns sticking our heads out the window, taking a breath and holding it while we waited for our next turn. I remember looking at the ladder below and debating if I could jump to it. A few of the guys threw their helmets out the window, the universal signal that firefighters are trapped above. I felt weak and sleepy. Images of Peggy and our kids came to me. I could see their faces clearly.

Some of the guys were weighing the possibility of sliding down the hose, but I knew I didn't have the strength. I suppose they considered it better than burning to death up there.

The fire in the clock room directly above us was raging. A ladder company was trying to reach us by pushing a thirty-five foot ladder over a hundred foot aerial ladder. To this day I don't know how they did it. When they reached the flat part of the roof, they manually raised the ladder trying to reach our location. A brother will do that for a brother.

I was sitting with my back toward the outside wall and was now breathing smoke, when suddenly the smoke lifted and we could breathe. This old clock had counter balance weights as large as ash buckets. The fire had burnt through the hanging supports and they came crashing through the ceiling above us. They were cherry red from heat and smashed through the catwalk in front of us. We made our way single file along what was left of the catwalk to the other side. I was holding onto the belt of the man in front of me; there was now fire below us on both sides of the cat walk. A Rescue Company met us and led out to an outside fire escape. Behind us the fire had come up the wooden stairs and engulfed the room with the circular window. We asked Captain Zook what we should do about the hose. "To hell with the hose," he said, "abandon ship!"

I guess from the street below it looked like we were gone. When we reached the street, my knees were shaking quite a bit.

The fire was eventually controlled and extinguished. When the fire vented, most of the heat and smoke dissipated. The fire walls held. They asked for volunteers to go up there again and a crew did re-enter the building. I did not volunteer. Harvard was very happy that we were able to save the structure, which is to this day one of the most magnificent buildings on campus.

The next day when Chief O'Connell picked up the morning reports he asked me what I thought of the fire. "It was a real toilet paper fire, Chief, " I said. "I nearly shit my pants!"

Memorial Hall is located across from Cambridge Fire Headquarters, and for the remainder of my career every time I looked at the building I could hear angels' wings.

The Wiz

Tom worked with me when I was stationed at Engine 5 in Inman Square. We all knew that he was smart and obviously had an education. He could speak intelligently, sometimes impressively, on many subjects—but his knowledge in front of a television set was what truly amazed us.

There was a quiz show on in the evening that we usually watched if things were quiet. The show involved complicated questions about such topics as art, literature, history, and foreign countries. When the TV show host asked the questions, Tom placed his hand to his forehead as if he were in deep thought and time after time he would come up with the correct answer. We were truly astonished by his breadth of knowledge and told him that he should write to the show's producers in New York to see how he could become a contestant. He would just sit there and grin and we would just shake our heads.

One afternoon our quiz show wiz-kid was on detail to another station. We had just had a new, more powerful TV antenna installed up on the roof and our reception was vastly improved. We even got stations from Rhode Island and New Hampshire. I was flicking the dial of the TV looking for something decent to watch when...*there it was*—the same show that we would be watching later on that evening!

Tom lived in New Hampshire! He would see the show before he came to work!

Later, when the night crew came in, I informed them of my discovery. What made the cheese more binding was the fact that from time to time Tom would take a bet that his answer would be right; he would *never* get the last floor patrol. We decided that a lesson was required.

The next time we worked together, we broke the exciting news: Bobby had written to the quiz show and explained why we felt that New Hampshire Tom should be a contestant on the show. The look on Tom's face was worth it all. He didn't know whether to cry or to scream. We told Tom that it was a great opportunity for him to make lots of money and to be a credit to the Cambridge Fire Department. Everything was arranged. There'd be no problem getting time off, the lieutenant said; he would explain everything to the chief as soon as we heard from the show. Everything would be fine. We'd even draw out the best route to drive to New York. And I'd go with him, I told Tom, if I could get the time off too. It would be swell.

Tom just sat there and became paler by the minute. Finally, it was time for the quiz show. As the host asked each question, I beat him to the punch line; the third time I did it Tom caught on and blurted out the truth. We just looked straight ahead and said nothing.

Tom never pulled that stunt again. In fact, he was very quiet when we watched TV.

A Little Help Please

I was company directory for the Relief Association when I was stationed at Inman Square. Each year I used to canvas the district and visit business establishments for donations to the Relief. This money was used to help defray medical expenses for the members and to assist the members' families when necessary. In those days the city or the insurance company did not cover all medical expenses.

A Chinese laundry operated in a building across from the fire station. It was a family affair, which back then meant that the entire family lived in the back rooms of the shop. They were hard working people who kept mostly to themselves. Knowing their circumstances I never bothered them to make a donation or to buy a ticket to the ball. When I walked into the store Tommy would say, "No tickee...No tickee!" I used to chuckle at that since I hadn't even asked him to donate.

One evening I was sitting at the patrol desk when a Cambridge police officer came in and said, "It's the damnedest thing I have ever seen!" When I asked what he was talking about, he responded that the Chinaman in the laundry across the street was caught in the transom. We walked across the street and sure enough, there Tommy was, caught in the transom over the front door. I guess the family members weren't home and he had locked himself out. His little legs were thrashing and he was really glad to see us.

I couldn't resist it. Taking the tickets out of my pocket, I asked Tommy if he would like to buy a ticket to the Cambridge firefighters' annual ball. "Oh yes, oh yes!" he replied. "I buy two tickets!"

We got a step ladder from the station and had Tom safely in his store in no time. We wouldn't take any money from him, but every year if he saw me, even if I was across the street, he'd run over and say, "I buy ticket, please!"

A Hand out the Window

I had been sick with the flu for about four days. It had gone through the entire family—first the kids, then Peggy, and now me. Sully told me to forget the watch and go to bed. I thanked him for his generosity, had a bowl of chicken soup and crackers and turned in.

Maybe I shouldn't have come to work, but we often did things like that. It was a cold and snowy night, the kind that you hope you can stay in. Sully was doing my watch and if he ever needed me I would be there for him.

The box came in about three a.m. The fire was in North Cambridge and we hoped they wouldn't need us. Bob shook the pole and said, "Engine 9 just reported heavy smoke showing." Now we all started to get ready since we took the run on the second alarm. Then we heard, "C-3 to Fire Alarm...C-3 to Fire Alarm...order of Chief Lally...strike second alarm Box 7229."

"OK, C-3. On the orders of Chief Lally, striking second alarm on city Box 7229."

The alert tone was now sounding but there was no need of it—we were already sliding down the poles and manning the apparatus. Out into the cold and snowy night we went. The first bite of the frigid wind almost took my breath away. It was my turn on the rear step and I turned my back to the wind, but it still was biting cold.

The lieutenant ordered us to drop a line. The fire was in the second floor of an occupied four story dwelling. People were being taken out over ladders. We could see heavy smoke coming from under the eaves and knew the fire was spreading fast. We were ordered to reduce the two and a half to one and a half and take the line over a ladder and into a third floor corner window.

I grabbed the pipe and threw it over my shoulder. The ladder guys had already been up there and taken out the window. They used a small dog chain to secure the ladder to the sill so it wouldn't slip. When I reached the window I could already feel the heat. My right knee was on the sill and all I had to do was pull myself in. Maybe the ladder slipped a little...I'm honestly not sure what happened...but I suddenly lost my balance. The air tank on my back seemed to be pulling me off the ladder. A weakness poured over me and getting into the window was now impossible.

Then I was falling and the images of my kids and my wife passed before me and then suddenly a very strong hand reached out of the smoke and with one pull I was in the window and on the floor. Through the facepiece of my mask I said, "Thanks, Jake! I owe you one." Jimmy Norton was in the room with me. It was getting hot. My ears were starting to burn.

The line was finally charged and we directed it up towards the ceiling to cool things down. The door in front of us was outlined in flame. "Jim, we're not going to be able to stay here, " I said, "it's getting ready to blow." He got back on the ladder and I handed him the nozzle.

The heat was now almost unbearable. Thick black smoke now allowed me to see nothing. The guy who saved me from falling was still in the room and I called for him to get the hell out, that it's time to leave. I knew flashover was imminent. From the ladder I made one last attempt to reach the guy, but I could feel nothing.

There was nothing left to do. We were half way down the ladder when the room blew and a ball of fire boiled out the window. If my saviour was still in there, he was gone. The fire went to four alarms with twenty-six people left homeless. My lieutenant told the chief officer of the incident and we went to the third floor room.

Only one staircase led to the room—with no other way out. He did not come down the ladder that we were on. We did not find a body and no firefighter was reported missing. All members were questioned and no one said that they had been in that room.

I cannot explain what happened at that fire. All that I know is that someone pulled me into the window and saved my life.

A Hand Too Far

For some reason Wednesdays were usually quiet; even the false alarms seemed to come in early, between 7:00 and 11:00 p.m. So Wednesday was a good night for drill time, a good opportunity to review the use of equipment, routes to box locations, and first aid to the injured. On this Wednesday evening we were just starting our drill when the box came in. I was very happy when the alarm sounded; I figured our drill time would be cut short and that by the time we returned to quarters the lieutenant would have forgotten about the drill.

I was riding the rear step of the hose wagon. The smell of burning wood was strong as we turned onto Broadway. Even though I could find no sign of fire, the smell of painted wood burning meant that there was a fire somewhere. We were second engine in, and when I looked up Broadway I could see the companies dropping big lines. Lieutenant Cummings was kneeling up in the pump seat and indicating that we should drop a line. Reaching under the canvas deck cover, I grabbed a few folds of two and a half inch line.

The pump connected to the hydrant at the corner of Windsor and Broadway. In Cambridge finding a hydrant at an intersection is always a good bet. This section of the city has a combination of factories and residences. The wagon stopped in front of two and a half story dwelling. Heavy black smoke was showing from under the eaves of the roof. There was also a glow of fire in the second floor front room. We definitely had a job tonight. Weather would not be a factor on this mild October night.

Deputy Chief Leary was standing in front of the building and ordered us to advance an inch and a half line up the front stairs to the second floor. The first arriving engine company had taken a line into the first floor, and they were operating on fire in the cellar. The fire had already raced the walls and had broken out on the second floor. I took the pipe; the lieutenant and Billy were backing me up.

The all-service canister type mask that we used then was adequate for above grade operations. As I crawled up the stairs, the sound of the fire crackling in the walls and ceiling gave sure indication that fire was above us. The line was not charged yet; it is a great deal easier to get into position with a dry line and then call for water. The stairs were narrow and dirty. At first I could see where I was going, but soon visibility became zero. Now the stairs were turning to the right. A stack of newspapers partially blocked my way. Using my shoulder I was able to wedge by and continue up the stairs. There it was, heavy fire in front of me. Tongues of flame were licking across the ceiling toward me. The line was now charged and directed toward the ceiling, then we heard a voice yelling from below us: "Back out! Back out!" The line was being pulled back. Pieces of the ceiling were falling down on top of us. I don't know why I did—maybe because we were taught to "give it one last sweep" before going back—but before descending the stairs I put out my gloved hand and swept around. My hand felt a large hole in front of me. I reached across as far as I could, but could feel nothing. I crawled backwards until I felt the stairs with the tip of my boot. The hose was now being pulled down the stairs. The thumping noise on the roof was the ladder men cutting a hole to relieve the trapped flammable gases and allow the engine companies to advance and hold position.

The second alarm had been sounded and other companies were going into operation. We attempted to make the stairs, but fallen plaster and lathing made our advance impossible. We assisted in overhauling the first floor area and checking the walls for hidden fire.

Someone was yelling up on the second floor that they had found a body and needed a body bag. The building had been used as a rooming house. The body of a middle-aged man was found just on the other side of the hole that I had encountered. His lifeless hand was outstretched. My hand must have missed him by inches. Later we were informed that most of the roomers were workers from Lever Brother Soap factory; several of them were immigrants. Soon we were dismissed from the fire.

We made up our line and returned to quarters. I was really troubled by that hand. If I had only stretched mine a little further...If only ...if only a few more inches...if only. Sleep did not come to me that night. I tossed and turned. Finally I left my bunk and went downstairs. Leo was on floor patrol and I offered to finish his watch. He made me a cup of coffee and brought it down. He knew I was troubled.

As I stood at the window and looked out at the dark square, my mind kept saying, "Who was he? Where was he from? Did he have family here?" and, of course, "If only I had...If only I...If only...."

A Night at the Bucket

From the kitchen window on the second floor of the firehouse I could see it all. Even for a Saturday night, *this* was a fight. Carey, the beat cop in the Square, had Kincade across the bar. Blood was flying all over the place. Kincade was putting up a pretty good fight, but in the end he was no match for Carey.

I didn't see it start, but I sure saw it finish. Now Kincade had Carey up over his head and he was twirling him around and around. Officer Carey was yelling at the other officers that he would make the arrest himself. It didn't look quite that way to me. At any minute I fully expected Officer Carey to be thrown through the plate glass window.

Now they were both on the floor and Carey had the upper hand in that he had an Irish sleeping wand—sometimes called a nightstick—and was throwing stardust into Kincade's eyes. Then it was over; Kincade was in the wagon on his way to the police station, complaining about his sore head and yelling that Carey doesn't fight fair. He would sleep it off and be none the worse in the morning.

The strange thing about this fight was that when I first came on duty I saw Carey and Kincade across the street talking like two old pals. Kincade wasn't a bad sort of guy; he worked as a laborer down at the city yard and when he was sober you could not ask for a nicer guy. Later that night I heard what had caused the fight. Kincade had hit his girlfriend, "Holy Mary", in the mouth. She was probably trying to persuade him to go home but he would have no part of it. Kelly, the bartender, informed Kincade that he ran a classy establishment and he would not tolerate such behavior. Kincade took exception when Kelly shut him off and called the police. They told me that he reached across the bar, picked Kelly up by his collar and punched him in the nose. Officer Carey was across the street and quick to respond.

At about five-foot-nine, Kincade was not a big man, but he was built like a steamroller. Officer Carey stood well over six feet and used to swim around Boston Harbor on his days off; he was in good shape.

When all the excitement was over I was sitting at the patrol desk downstairs when Officer Carey walked in. He was covered with blood, and I don't think it was his own. "Obie, can I use your phone to call the station? I have to tell them that I have to go home and change my uniform shirt." He was one tough cop who watched over his little part of the world. He knew everyone in that square by their first name and could solve many problems in his own way.

Many a youth Carey caught doing wrong rode the tips of his shoe and had trouble sitting down for a time. One Christmas I saw him open the trunk of his patrol car, look around to make sure that no one was watching, then he called a woman over to the car and handed her a large cardboard box full of food.

Even though he didn't have a family of his own, he loved to talk about the kids. When I would tell him about my baby, I could see his eyes light up. Many a frigid winter's night I would look down at the square and see Officer Carey walking his beat and checking to see that doors were locked. He's gone now, but I am sure that Cambridge is a better place because of him.

Another memorable incident that involved the police occurred when Okie, the local bookie, ran into the firehouse one night and started stuffing betting slips into his mouth. He was looking frantically out the window and yelling, "Hide me! Hide me!" With that he ran into the back room. **Bang!** The front door opened and there stood three angry Cambridge Police Officers. "Which way did he go?" one of them bellowed. Remaining strictly neutral, I replied with a shrug.

Okie made good his escape and I was give a stern warning

about the penalty for harboring a criminal. I spent the rest of the day wondering if Okie had eaten my slip and if my number had come in. It didn't.

The Missing Horses

The weather reports all said that the hurricane would hit our area about noon. It was now ten a.m. and already the wind was picking up.

An extra group was told to report for overtime duty. The only problem was that in those days there was no such thing as overtime pay. Duty was duty and they could call us any time the need presented itself. The standard responses to complaints about this practice went something like "Well, we have a list, you know. So just quit."

An MTA bus driver came into quarters and reported that trolley wires were down one block up Cambridge Street. Captain Danworth told Bill and me to block off the street with wooden horses. This we did.

The bus driver returned to the station a little later and again told the captain that we better get there and block the street off.

"I told you two blockheads to block the damned street off!" the captain screamed at us. "No go *do* it!"

"Cap, we did, Cap, we swear," we tried to argue, but up the street we went again. Now the wind was really blowing. We saw why the horses had galloped away—the wind took them. Back we go to the firehouse and Capt. Danforth to report the fact that the horses were gone with the wind.

The captain understood, of course, and that was that....*Wrong!* Once again the bus driver entered the station and started giving the captain hell for not properly protecting the public. Well, the one thing that you do not is accuse the boss of not protecting the public. He loudly explained to the guy in no uncertain terms exactly where he could go. He was standing so close to the guy that as he spoke he was spitting all over the guy's glasses.

We next received a call for a tree down against a house on Fayette Street. Trees were blocking a section of the street and we had to walk. When we arrived at the scene, the tree leaned against the house and live wires were scattered all over the place. About all we could do was put in a call for Boston Edison and tell everyone to stay away from the wires. Edison, naturally, was very busy and it was quite some time before they had someone on the scene. Finally, two workmen arrived and killed the power.

The rain was now coming down hard, a torrential downpour. On the way back to quarters we passed the trolley wires and spotted where we'd put the horse. The wires were still live and very dangerous. The same MTA driver who made the initial report was standing in the street with a flashlight keeping the cars away. The police were also very busy and would be delayed in responding.

We positioned the pump so that no traffic could come near and stood by. When the electric power was finally cut off, the bus driver thanked us for all we did and had attempted to do.

The next call we received was for overhead trolley wires down and laying on top of a coal truck. When we arrived a cop was pointing to the truck and saying, "They're both dead." We'd been told that two men were in the coal truck, so I assumed the police officer was talking about the occupants. Wires were arcing against the metal side. When I walked around the truck, I could see two men inside; they were very much alive...and very, very frightened. Coal dust covered their faces. One man clenched a small pipe in his mouth; his eyes were as big as saucers. The other fellow fingered his beads as he said his prayers. When I asked them if they are all right, they replied in very heavy Irish brogues that they were but to "Get us the hell outta this godforsaken truck!" The Rescue responded and used rubber gloves and a big wire cutter to snap the wires. The two coal men were now free and wasted no time leaving the scene.

It was very fortunate that they did not try to get out of the truck. The rubber tires kept the truck insulated from the ground. With the live wires arcing against the truck, all they had to do was step on the ground and it would have been all over.

The Hat

At long last I was to be issued a new uniform hat. To me it seemed I'd waited forever. The hat I'd been issued over three years ago and which I was still wearing was beginning to show very serious signs of wear.

In those days we were required to wear the uniform to and from the job. If you had the floor patrol, you wore the full uniform. This stipulation was later changed and you were required to wear the work uniform while on floor patrol. The wearing of the uniform hat, however, was never changed. We kept a spare black tie near the watch desk but you needed your own hat.

The day had finally arrived. Deputy Chief Burke presented my new hat to me in the morning. It was really something, all new with a lovely black, shiny visor—a beauty among hats. That afternoon I had the two to four housewatch. I sat at the patrol desk looking so good, I thought, in my new hat. The bells started to ring—Box 291—it's a run for us. Off went my new hat and I placed it where I was sure it would be perfectly safe, on the knob at the top of the banister. Down the pole they slid, one after the other.

I never did find out who did it—who knocked my hat off the post and allowed it to land under the wheels of the very hose wagon *I* was driving. Oh misery! I felt the slight bump as I drove out the door. No time to stop, just time to worry. Was that my hat I felt under the wheels? Couldn't be, no way, because I had placed it where it would be safe.

The run was a confounded false alarm, so we returned to quarters pretty quickly. As I approached the ramp and turned to back in, I saw it, my hat, my shiny, new hat, as flat as a pancake. My worst fears had been realized.

My heart sank. I had run over my new hat. I stopped the hose wagon on the apron and walked up to the spot and looked down at my brand new hat. The lieutenant came up and stood beside me. "Gee, Connie," he said, "that hat sure is flat." I felt a tear in the corner of my eye.

It was gone. I now had no new hat. After picking up its remains I am so distraught that I almost hit the wall as I backed the wagon into the firehouse. As I step onto the floor I yell, "OK, OK who knocked my new hat on the floor!" No reply; everyone's silence denied their responsibility. Then Bill said, "Lighten up, Connie, and just put in for a new one. All you have to do is explain it was your negligence for putting the foolish hat where you did in the first place."

The next night we were on duty the chief's driver, Dick Stang, came into quarters and said to me, "Connie, I hear you lost your hat and it was given a nice funeral!"

"Never mind the bullshit, Stang," I replied.

"You know, I'm in good graces with the chief who's in charge of supply. I can get you another hat without any of the paperwork."

This was music to my ears. "Gee, Dick, if you could it'd be great! I take a seven and a quarter."

For three months I waited—no hat. Every time I saw him I would ask, "Hey, Dick, where's my new hat?" and he would always reply, "Connie, old pal, it's coming, trust me, it's coming." I trusted and waited. Still no hat.

We had roll call in those days. Both the relieving and the relieved groups would line in front of the apparatus as General Orders and special notices were read. Since I didn't have a hat of my own, I'd been borrowing one from a guy who was off duty. After roll call one day the captain told me he wanted to see me in his office. "O'Brien, where is your uniform hat?" I told him the whole, painful story. He just leaned back and shook his head. "Connie, Dick Stang is only kidding you. He has no friends who'll give you another new hat." He then told me the only thing I could do was go over to Linsky Uniform and buy a new hat. So I purchased a new hat and was very careful not to damage it.

I confronted Dick the next time we met and told him what the captain had said. "It's not true, Connie, not true at all!" he responded. The next day we were on duty Dick came into quarters and handed me a new hat: "No paperwork, Connie," he said, "just like I said. No paperwork, OK?"

Dick Stang was seriously injured at a fire several years later. He was coming out of a building and slipped on ice on the stairs. He received a very serious back injury from which he never recovered. For years before the accident every time I saw him I'd say, "Hey, Dick, I still have my hat!" He'd laugh and say, "That's good, Connie. Glad it still fits." Years later I learned that he had, in fact, gone in town and bought me the hat.

I wore many hats during my forty-two year career, but I will never forget that particular one, the hat that Dick gave me.

A Fish Story

The chief and his aide had just picked up the morning reports at Engine 5. The next stop would be at the East Cambridge station, Engine 3 and Ladder 2. It was a hot, sultry day in August that promised to get only hotter. As they waited for the light to change, a woman in the car next to them glared conspicuously at them. The light turned green, however, and they were on their way again.

"Bobby, I wonder what that lady was staring at?"

"Gee, Chief, I don't know. Maybe she think she knows you."

At the next light the same thing happened, only this time it was a man staring at them. He had a very distressed look on his face, as if he were in pain. The chief stared back at him and the man just shook his head.

"Bobby, do you smell something?"

"You know, Chief, I do. It smells like fish. I wasn't going to mention it 'cause I thought maybe Ida made you a sandwich for lunch or something."

Soon they were pulling up on the ramp of the East Cambridge station...and so was the smell. Bobby got out of the car and stood there shaking his head. "I'll be damned, Chief, I think we're the ones that stink." They were both outside now looking at the car.

"That smell's coming from underneath!" the chief huffed.

"Gee, Chief, I don't remember driving in any salt water but it sure smells like fish to me."

By this time a small group of curious citizens had gathered on the ramp; they are all staring at the car. This firehouse is located across the street from the Middlesex Courthouse. The lieutenant of Ladder 2 came out and suggested to the chief that the investigation continue inside the privacy of station.

Bobby slid under the car and called back that all was well underneath. They next raised the hood and lo and behold, they discovered the culprit. Although they had not driven in the ocean, nevertheless, a rather large and partly cooked haddock was wired to the manifold.

"Oh, lord!" mutters the chief.

"Oh shit!" cries Bobby.

The lieutenant began laughing.

The perpetrator turned out to be the resident clown and prankster of Engine 5—who was also an avid fisherman.

The chief, who was due at a safety meeting in a half hour, was livid. The shop provided another vehicle, the car was returned to Five's house and the clown spent the rest of the day scraping dried fish off the manifold.

Mr. Clown also spent a noisy afternoon session behind the closed door of the deputy's office.

Cut by Glass

The fire was in a large tenement house in the neighboring town of Somerville. We covered Somerville Engine 3 on the second alarm, and by the sound of the radio we would not be there long. The first thing a covering company does is check out the kitchen refrigerator for goodies left over from dinner. My hand was on the door of the fridge when the phone rang and the lieutenant was told to respond to the fire.

As we pulled out of the station, the big city gongs were striking the third alarm. I could see a glow in the night sky ahead. It was summer and there were many spectators, even at one a.m. After reporting to the chief in front of the building, we were ordered to advance a big line over a thirty-five foot ladder into the third floor window.

Bill was on the pipe and I had a bite of hose on my shoulder. The fire in the room had been pretty well knocked down, but there was still a heavy smoke condition. Bill used the pipe to break the glass in the window; some of it smashed down on my helmet. We know enough to keep our heads down. Then I felt a sharp stab on my wrist. No time to investigate now—Billy was already in the room and pulling in more line. The deck guns were still working somewhere; I could hear the water striking the ceilings and walls. Conditions inside were not really that bad. Visibility through my Scott Air face mask was good. Then the guns were shut down; heavy stream appliances normally halt when interior operations begin.

I noticed that my right hand felt sticky. When I pulled the glove off, I discovered a cut on my wrist, a cut that was bleeding pretty good. *Hmmmmm.* However, I decided this was not the time to give any attention to a cut, put the glove back on my hand, and back to work I went. No lousy cut was going to stop me from working at this fire. The ladder guys opened the walls and ceilings and we hit the fire as it became exposed. Every once in a while I checked the burning sensation in my wrist. It was still bleeding. *Hmmmmm.*

A chief ordered us down to take a blow. In the rear yard, I bummed a cigarette off a jake and lit up. Time to check the wrist. Still bleeding—*hmmmmm!* Over an hour had passed since I'd been cut. You'd think the bleeding would have stopped by now. Why's my heading feeling so strange...so light...I'm OK...I'm-uh...OK.

The ride to the hospital was uneventful except for the fact that the police officer driving the paddy wagon had difficulty keeping the vehicle in gear. He held his foot on the gear shift. The doctor asked me how long I'd been bleeding like that. They are taking my blood pressure—there is none. The table is tilting. My head is down and my feet are up. *Hmmmmm.* I hear them talking about shock. I tell them that I was nowhere near an electric line. The doctor begins crocheting on my wrist and I hear someone mention a blood transfusion. I hope they don't expect me to donate any—I gave my share.

Now other people are in the emergency room. They were injured occupants of the fire building. One man had badly cut feet from walking on glass. The other two were suffering from smoke inhalation. After about an hour a nurse took my blood pressure again; it was normal. Before he discharged me, the doctor had a few kind words to say to me about not going to the hospital when I should have, then the chief's aide gave me a ride back to Engine 5.

I was on injured leave for two tours. When I came back to work I head that on the way back to the fire the Somverville paddy wagon caught fire. It seems the transmission overheated. Lt. Malvern informed me that the City of Somerville was suing the City of Cambridge for the cost of repair. He also said that since the City of Cambridge was so broke, they planned on attaching my salary for fifty cents each week.

"Nice try, Lute," I said, "nice try."

Washing Windows

We washed the windows of the firehouse on Friday mornings unless it was raining. Sometimes we tried letting the hose run down the glass from the second floor so that when the lieutenant looked up from his crossword puzzle he might think it was raining. Sometimes we'd shake a piece of tin for a thunder effect. It never worked. As Christmas approached, we would use Bonami to decorate the apparatus door windows with various seasonal designs. We really looked forward to doing this—it meant that the windows would not have to be washed for weeks. One morning it was my turn to wash the windows in the captain's office. I sat on the window sill with my back outside the window, pulled the top sash down to my lap and started washing. However, the sash weight must have slipped because when I went to open the window it was jammed tight across my thighs.

Just then the bells started ringing for a church fire. Holy smoke, we were first due into the box. Desperately I wiggled and tried to free myself, but to absolutely no avail. My company responded without me as I waved my cleaning rag at them.

A covering company finally released me from my prison and I responded to the fire. When I told the lieutenant what had happened, he just shook his head and said, "Connie, you would screw up a high mass!"

Rooming House

Charlie's eyes would always give him away. He was sitting at the table with a pat hand and was refusing to make a bid.

"Come on, partner," I said. "How 'bout a little help!"

"You play hour hand, Obie, and I'll play mine," he replied.

In five minutes the eleven o'clock news would be on and that would be the end of the whist game anyway. Just then a box began coming in. It was being struck for a rooming house on Cottage Street. That was the end of the card game—out we went. The smell of burning leaves permeated the air and the traffic wasn't bad at all. We turned into Cottage and the lieutenant indicated that he wanted me to drop a line from the wagon. Now I could see it. The smoke was banked down on the street and a company was advancing a line up the front stairs.

The chief ordered us to take a line over a twenty-four foot ladder and into a second floor window. Naturally the structure is loaded with people; after all, it's a rooming house. On the roof of the porch beneath the second floor Charlie was putting on his mask. His very thin face sometimes made getting a proper seal difficult. Up on the third floor was a guy in his underwear sitting on the window sill yelling that he's going to jump. Charlie kept yelling at him to stay there, that he'd be right up there to save him. Either the guy was being burnt or he never heard Charlie because jump he did. He nearly hit both us as he struck the porch gutter and landed in the bushes below.

Charlie now began seriously berating the jumper: "You stupid bastard, I told you not to jump, that we were coming!

Now look at you! You idiot! Did ya think we were lying to you!"

Once we stepped inside the room I could feel the heat. We made our way to the hall and started hitting the visible fire. As we advanced the line up the stairs from the second to the third floor, scalding hot water cascaded down on us. This was the water that we were playing on the flames now coming back at us as steam. Ladder men above us were cutting a four foot by four foot hole in the roof to let some of the smoke and heat out.

Charlie had the mask on; I didn't. In those days we didn't have enough masks to go around. A man was judged and rated by the amount of smoke he could take. I was keeping my head close to the floor because some air came in with the water. The bulk of the fire was knocked down. Chief Kelly told us to go down and take a blow. I walked down the side stairs, making my way over and under lathing and charged lines. The minute I hit the fresh air on the porch it was like floating away.

Someone was holding a capsule of smelling salts under my nose. I realize I'm in the Rescue wagon and that other guys are being loaded into the wagon. Some were in bad shape. The side door was open. I sat up and kept sliding down to make room for other firefighters. Shrugging off the blanket and oxygen mask, out the door I stepped. The cool autumn air felt good against my face. I saw Charlie rolling up hose down the street. Lieutenant Malvern asked me if I was OK. In the back yard I started to roll up hose. The only problem was that I kept falling over the hose and landing on my back looking up at the full Harvest Moon. Soon we were ordered to return to our own quarters. While passing though Central Square, sitting on top of the wet hose, a strange feeling came over me. I was starting to float away again. I hung on tight to the crossbar until we finally arrived at the station. When I hopped down to open the doors my legs sure felt strange.

I was off the next two days and stayed at home and rested up. My poor mother wondered why I kept spitting up that black gook.

The day I returned to the firehouse, I was cleaning the hose wagon when Captain Ryder, the captain of the Rescue Company, came into quarters looking for me. If I live to be one hundred years of age, I will never forget the brutal tongue lashing Captain Ryder gave me.

"Listen to me, kid, you were slated to be transported to the hospital with the rest of them guys for severe smoke inhalation. Did you *know* that!" He was now thumping my chest with his finger; I was getting the point and trying to answer but he kept it up, gaining momentum. "If you ever pull a stupid, idiotic stunt like that again, I *will* put you up on charges." He turned and walked away, almost breaking the glass as he slammed the door.

I returned to my wagon with his words still ringing in my ears. They had a nickname for him—"Donkey Rider." Captain Ryder was an excellent firefighter and a most compassionate man. He knew the true dangers of smoke inhalation and was looking out for my welfare. And since I can *still* look back on that incident and shake my head at my own professional innocence, I guess Captain Ryder did his job pretty well.

Put Out My Pillow

About three o'clock one morning a guy came to the station and rang the emergency bell. When a firefighter asked what the problem was, the fellow replied, "Will you guys put out the fire in my pillow?" He is asked where he got the pillow. "From the car," he responded. He is next asked where the car is located, to which he replied, "Up the street." One of the guys stepped out onto the apron, looked up street, and all he could see was fire.

It seems the fellow got a little drunk, fell asleep in the car, set the car on fire, which was parked next to his house, so the house went up too. It took two alarms to put all the fires out. The police put him up for the remainder of the night. I don't think they allowed the pillow in the cell.

We later learned that he was afraid to go into his house if he was drunk. His father had been known to beat him up, and his mother would call the police.

Dinner

We had a fellow who was a spark and would ride with us occasionally. He worked for a rendering company, picking up meat trimmings. Every Thursday he'd show up at the firehouse with a nice chunk of beef for the boys. We'd cook a nice meal—roast beef dinner, mashed potatoes, a couple of vegetables. It was the rookie's responsibility to get the rolls and desert at Hart's Bakery across the street from the station.

Lieutenant Malvern would sit down and say, "To hell with the potatoes—I can get them at home. Pass me the meat." When the meal was finished they would sit around and pick their teeth until someone finally asked, "How much is this dinner costing us anyway?" They would sit there and complain about the cost until someone said, "Come one, come on...let's clean up!" Then it started: "Well, I cooked so I don't wash dishes." It seemed everyone was a damned cook, so guess who ended up washing the dishes! The rookie, me!

It was not at all unusual that after cooking the meal and just as we were about to sit down, an alarm would come in and we would have a fire. When we returned a covering company would be leaving quarters, usually wearing big smiles on their faces. We'd find a note upstairs thanking us for the meal and stating they were so sorry they had to leave without washing the dishes.

I remember one particular gentleman was a real grunge who worked for the city as a garbage collector. This guy had a name like poet or a composer should have—Mark Tifley. At this time

"Holy Mary" was Mark's girlfriend. These two lovebirds would stand in front of the fire station and argue and fight. She would beat him up every time. He never, never won. I guess in their own way they were in love.

We had just finished cooking a meal one Saturday when we responded to a working fire; we were gone for about an hour. When we returned, there sat Mark and Holy Mary, just finishing our dinner. It seems the cop on the beat, Officer O'Connor, had invited them to partake of our feast. We boiled the dishes for two hours. Then we decided to throw them away. O'Connor almost fell off the chair laughing.

One week we decided to cook a turkey for our Sunday meal. The vegetables were just about done and the turkey was waiting in the oven when we get a call to respond to the city dump...to spend the afternoon! The fire was burning over about a four block area and we were one of five companies fighting it. The danger was the fire spreading to houses on New Street. We were stretching lines down a bank of trash when over the radio we heard a box striking for smoke coming out of the windows of our fire station. Bill looked at me and quietly asked, "Did you shut off the oven?"

Well, the turkey and the stove were destroyed and we washed walls for weeks per order of the captain.

Ring Any Bell

It was one of those cold and miserable New England winter nights. It had been snowing earlier, but now it was just cold. We were the detail company at what was left of a furniture warehouse on Massachusetts Avenue in North Cambridge.

There wasn't much left of the warehouse. Usually the detail will be a company that is not in the district and not at the three alarm fire. Engine 5 had been at another call at the time, so we caught the detail. Ladder 4 was with us for part of the night but returned to quarters about three a.m.

Bill Mcall and I were sitting on the deck of Five's wagon operating the deck gun. We were both wet and cold. The Sally Wagon (the Salvation Army Canteen Truck) had left the scene over an hour ago, taking the warmth of their coffee with them. The spray of the gun had frozen on our helmets and coats and we looked like some sort of ice creatures.

Captain Barry told us to take a break and sent two other guys to sit with the gun. The only problem was there was just nowhere to go to get out of the cold. Back in those days most of the apparatus had open cabs and the pump operator had trouble keeping warm. We were numb with cold.

Half a block up the street was a row of apartment houses. We picked one only to discover that the door was locked. "Ring any goddam bell, " I chattered to Bill. "Let's get to hell out of this cold."

The door buzzer sounded, we pushed the door and we were inside the hallway. *Warmth!* It was wonderful. We sat on the marble stairs and Bill began searching for a dry cigarette to smoke. I searched my pockets but my cigarettes were all soaked and ruined. Bill finally found one but the matches were wet. I suggested he ring another bell and ask for a match. He did, but he received no response.

We just sat there minding our business, appreciating the small bit of warmth we'd found, when a police cruiser pulled up in front of the building. It seems our hosts had banned together and reported to the police that some strange looking bums had entered the hallway and were ringing the door bells.

As we were explaining to the two cops that we were just trying to stay out of the cold for a little while, one of the residents, an elderly woman, opened the interior door. The police explained to the woman the reported bums were actually just a couple of Cambridge firefighters. "Well, that may be," she said, "but they are so dirty and smell of burnt wood." The officers then took us into their cruiser. At least it was warm in the car—and we got a smoke!

They drove us back to the fire and advised us to stay out of strange doorways. We thanked them for their hospitality and a dry match.

A Little Brass Polish

Every Saturday was brass day on both floors; every bit of brass work was shined. We had a newly promoted deputy chief in our district and he wore a brand new suit with brass buttons on the front of his coat. One Saturday he came into quarters on an inspection tour, and the lieutenant invited him up to the second floor for a cup of coffee.

My task was to shine the sliding pole. Placing the step ladder against the pole, I applied the polish. They used to call me "the Noxon Kid." Unfortunately, I forgot to yell up and warn the men on the second floor.

Naturally an alarm came in and down the pole slid the new deputy chief. The ladder was knocked over, landed on the pumper's windshield and cracked it. The chief responded to the call with a green stripe right down between his brass buttons.

After the mess was cleaned up, the lieutenant said that I had better hide; I spent the remainder of the tour hiding behind the coal pile. The chief never mentioned the incident, even though I am sure his uniform coat was ruined.

A Voice from Below

Until the day I die I will swear that there is gold under the streets of Cambridge because every time you look around some city department or public utility company like Edison or Boston Gas is digging up the street. And it's never a quiet street that few people travel, and it's always been this way.

One summer's day a crew from the gas company began digging in front of our apparatus door. The gas company was laying new lines. This posed a problem because we were forced to use only one door in responding to and returning from alarms. On the second or third day of the excavation project, Bill Mcall and I were repairing hose in the cellar when I noticed you could hear voices from the trench in front of quarters. The hose bench was right against the front wall and the voices were coming through old phone lines in the foundation.

As the gas company's laborers dug in their hole their voices sounded very Irish to me and Bill. Leaning close to the opening I made a *Oh-oooooo* sound and the talking stopped. I repeated the sound.

"What's that now?" a voice said. "Do you hear it?"

"Hear what?" his co-worker answered.

"Can't you hear the voice callin'?"

"You know, Pat, I think you've been workin' too hard—too much overtime, you know."

Oh-ooooooooo! I groaned, just a bit more loudly.

"My God, man, I do hear it now, I do!"

Oh-oooooooo!

"Who is dat makin' dat noise?" he asked.

Just then we had a run which turned out to be a false alarm; when we returned to quarters we told Lieutenant Malvern what we were up to. We all walked into the street and looked into the hole and asked what all the commotion was about. A very Irish face looked up at me from the ditch and said, "There is a voice in the hole, boy, and we don't know where it's coming from."

The lieutenant and Bill remained in position looking into the hole while I snuck back to the cellar to continue our conversation. *Oh-oooooooo!* I moaned; I added just a pinch of agony to my tone this time. "There tis again! Do You hear it, lad? Do you hear it? Who is dat callin'? Now answer me!"

Placing my mouth close to the hole, I replied, "The suffering souls of purgatory."

There was pause and then a reply in a low and quite sincere voice: "I pray for you people all the time, you know."

I just had to see what was going on from above so I returned to the trench and Bill went to the cellar. The lieutenant was leaning over the half-door, trying very hard not to laugh. Pat was out of the hole and arguing with his boss to come down and listen to the wall.

The bells started ringing and off we went to the report of a building fire on Hamlin Street. It was food on the stove with no duty, so we quickly returned to the ongoing Saga of the Trench. Now the two laborers and their foreman were in the ditch and having quite an argument. The foreman said that enough was enough and there was work to be done. Lieutenant Malvern said that we'd better stop or else the area would be declared a shrine and we'd have to re-locate the firehouse.

I returned to the cellar wall for one last time. "Hello! Hello! Can you hear me down there?"

"Yes, I can hear you," I replied. "Can you hear me?"

Pat now asked me who I was and what I wanted. He said the foreman wanted to know. Deciding it was time to finish this escapade, I replied that I was in China and if they dug any deeper they would be in my living room. Then I raced back up to the trench where I saw Pat reporting to the foreman what I had just said and the boss just shaking his head.

I've often wondered for how long the voice in the hole remained a mystery to Pat and his companions.

Lorrie's Emporium

Right next door to Engine 5 in Inman Square we had Lorrie's Restaurant. It was really some place to eat. Lorrie also owned a junk business that he ran when he was not cooking food. The junk trucks were parked outside the rear door. This was very handy for him because when someone came in he just got down from the truck and started cooking up the order. The only trouble for the customers was that to Lorrie it seemed a shame to wash his hand when he would soon return to the junk pile.

The food was good and the service better. The man never, never smiled. When you asked him how he was feeling, he'd begin with "Hey, kid, I'm really sick..." and then offer you a litany of ailments that were killing him. On Saturday nights when the bars in the area closed, Lorrie's was the place to head for. One time I asked him how often he washed the grill. He responded that every once in a while the grill would catch fire and the excess fat would burn off. I just shook my head. My favorite Lorrie preparation was his custard pudding—it was delicious. I never knew what was in it and I'm sure he didn't either.

One night about midnight I was sitting at the patrol desk. It was summer time and we had the apparatus doors open when suddenly the smell hit me like a ton of bricks; it was a combination of sewer gas and a garbage truck. Just then a patron rushed in and told me that there was a fire next door at Lorrie's. I called Fire Alarm and a box was transmitted. It was—of course—a grease fire; the heavy black smoke was hanging about three feet above the floor. We lugged our hose in the front door. The counter was still full of customers eating. The lieutenant began ordering everyone out but few of them actually moved. The smoke was so bad that I was crawling among people's feet on the floor.

Lorrie paid absolutely no attention to the fire as he asked a lady how she liked her home fries.. Glass was breaking and the fire was spreading. Lieutenant Malvern began pulling people out of the front door. It was total chaos. Shanahan, Lorrie's dishwasher, was pouring water on the burning grease. A lady was hitting Bill McCall over the head with a plate, the restaurant dog, Sparky, bit the deputy chief. Officer O'Reardon had just arrested Vinny Maginty for disturbing the peace. People were sitting on the running boards the apparatus, holding their plates and eating their eggs. Officer O'Toole had the wagon on the way. And Lorrie was yelling that there would a slight delay with the home fries.

Somehow, I don't really know how, the fire went out. Lorrie wanted to re-open the following Monday. He intended to use some of the same food. For some reason the Board of Health pulled his license, and Lorrie became a full time junk man.

The New England Brickyard Fire

At the turn of the century Cambridge was home to a thriving brick industry most of which was located in the northwest section of the city. Many of the people who worked in the brick factories were immigrants from Ireland and England. However, by the time I was appointed to the Cambridge Fire Department in the early 1950s, all that remained of this once bustling local business, for the most part, were abandoned sheds. In some case the clay vein gave out. In others, natural springs filled the pits with water. When I was a boy we used to swim in the water filled pits. You could stand on the chimney top and rest. The water was so clear that when we dove down we could see the roofs of the buildings.

My parents never gave me permission to swim at the "pit"; in fact, I was expressly forbidden to go anywhere near the pit—but on a hot day in the city the temptation was simply too great. A twelve year old girl did drown at the pit. Betty Powers dove in the area of the submerged buildings and did not come up. I wasn't there when it happened. I can remember my mother saying, "Connie, I'm glad you stay away from that place." I just looked away.

A few small companies were still baking bricks, and since the process involved the use of drying kilns, we did have serious fires there. One such fire occurred in the early 1950s. It was a Saturday and we were getting ready for our noon dinner. Henry, who worked at the rendering factory, had give us a nice piece of beef. I'd gone to Vincent's Market and picked up the vegetables, then to Hart's for bread and desert. The table was being set when we heard box 7816 being struck for a reported building fire in the abandoned section of the brickyard. Our ears went up because this area had a bad record. When Engine 4 pulled out on the apron, they reported heavy smoke in the distance; they were only part way up Rindge Avenue when they ordered a second alarm.

We were slated to go on the second alarm, so Bill McCall and I grabbed a knife and started to butter a few slices of bread for the trip uptown. As we raced up Beacon Street with the Federal sirens screeching, we could see why Engine 4 was getting excited. The sky was jet black. Once we reached Massachusetts Avenue it was a straight run. As we raced up the Avenue people stopped and stood still on the sidewalks and pointed at the sky. I could see flames shooting fifty feet into the air.

We took Rindge Avenue and the pump grabbed a hydrant on Sherman Street. The lieutenant was giving the hand signal to drop two big lines. We were going into deck gun operations. Even now the wind was starting to pick up. Clouds of brick dust were swirling toward the flames.

Charlie Mollar drove the hose wagon into the yard where a chief officer gave our lieutenant orders where he wanted to the gun to work. Three large wooden sheds were roaring; each shed was about 200' x 40' x 35' high; the sheds were separated from each other by a twenty foot railroad siding. The wind was now whistling by my ears. Chief Marvin indicated that he wanted the hose wagon to locate on the lee side and the deck gun trained on the rear porches of a string of three deckers (wood frame dwellings) that were becoming severely exposed. Large pieces of burning embers were flying through the air in the direction of the exposures. The lines were charged and snapped to life as the water rushed toward the gun. Now the question became how long would we be able to hold our position. We turned our helmets around backwards to break up the heat waves against our faces.

Bill and I were on the wagon deck moving the gun in a sweeping motion. The rusty water turned to steam before it could reach the exposed triple deckers. It was a losing effort. We had a good hydrant supplying us, but other companies had hooked up and were drawing water away from us.

The heat was the thing. My rubber coat started to smoke. I tucked my chin inside my coat because the air was getting too hot to breathe. We can't hold our position much longer, I thought. The fire was now four alarms. Our gun was useless. I wished that I had put my gloves on—my hands were burning. The damn gloves were in my rubber coat pocket and I was reaching for them when I heard someone yell, **"Get off the wagon!"** Bill and I jumped down and started running back up the tracks. Now there was blackness. No sound, just blackness. I could not breathe. A terrific weight was on my chest. And then someone was there beside me.

I can see him now. He is dressed in white. He is sitting in a chair and talking to me in a low reassuring voice. I tell him about my family, my three kids, and explain to him that I do not want to die. He just sat there, not looking directly at me, and said, "Yes, I know...I know...."

As we ran up the tracks I was closest to the burning shed. There was a loud rumble and the shed collapsed sideways toward the hose wagon. Bill had jumped to the other side and it didn't catch him. A section of the roof fell on top of me. It caught two other guys, Fairlawn and Souza, who had been operating a two and a half inch line but were now also running. They were found and removed quickly. I was not quite so lucky. Bill reported my approximate location under the debris and the Rescue crew dug me out. They had to use a battering ram to break through the foundation brick. What saved my life was the way the wall slid sideways, making a sort of shelter for me.

I wasn't alone in the hospital room. Every bone in my body hurt. Every one was in white. The oxygen mask was too tight against my face and I asked a nurse to move it. I had a ringing in my ears. The medical personnel were talking to me, but the damn ringing was making if difficult to understand them. The large green oxygen cylinder was close to my head. Someone was asking me how I felt. "Like the world fell on top of me!" I responded. Then things became clearer. I saw Peggy holding my hand and I noticed she was crying. I asked her how the kids were. She told me that I had been in the hospital for a day and a half.

I was suffering from severe smoke inhalation and various cuts and bruises; my full stay in the hospital lasted two weeks. Buddy Fairlawn was semi-conscious when the Rescue got to him; he was in a room down the hall from me. Souza escaped with a fractured collar bone. Two days later they put Buddy and me in the same room; shortly afterward they realized they'd made a mistake. The boys would come to see us and would raise a little good natured hell. Larry Keenan showed up with two of his lady friends, a six pack of beer and wanted to have a party. Larry was a bit distressed when the head nurse told him that he and his companions would have to leave. He told the nurse that he was a member of the Rescue team that had located us and we all should do a little celebrating. The head nurse explained to him again, in no uncertain terms, that this was a hospital not a pizza parlor. When she pointed him towards the door, Larry left in a huff, claiming loudly that he'd been "thrown outta better joints than this one, lady!"

Buddy was discharged after a week.

When it was time for me to leave the hospital I told Peggy that I wanted to thank the male nurse or doctor who was with me the first night. I thought it kind of strange that I didn't see the face again during my entire stay at the hospital. I pressed the issue and she told me that the only person in the ICU that first night was a female nurse and she had been far too busy to talk to me.

Ice on a Roof

We responded on the box alarm for a building fire on Third Street. It was a six story factory and going pretty good. Smoke was showing from the upper floors. The chief ordered us to get a line to the fifth floor. There was already one line in front of us up the front stairs. The smoke was so thick that you couldn't see your hand in front of your face. In those days it was not the common procedure to wear a smoke mask. I guess we rated each other on the amount of smoke a fire fighter could take before he collapsed.

Engine 8 was above us. They had made the fourth floor landing and I could hear the charged line working on the fire. I had the play pipe but we had not charged the line yet. We were backing up Eight. The lieutenant told me to check the controlling lever on the pipe to be sure that it was off. We had just got water when a tremendous blast of heat rushed down the stairs.

I had my head close to the stairs looking for a little air. The blast went right over my helmet. Looking up I could see the tongues of flame lapping on the wooden ceiling. Eight's crew was now beating a hasty retreat down the stairs. It was dark, hot and smokey. Fish Cakes and I kept the line operating on the ceiling to cover their retreat. My friend Bill Bergan on Engine 8 stumbled down on top of me and yelled, "I've seen God, Connie! Connie, I've seen God!" Bill didn't know it, but this factory manufactured large statues, especially the kinds one is likely to see in church, and there was a large statue of Christ on the fourth floor landing.

The fire now had the upper hand and they were yelling from below for us to get the hell out. Bill was still insisting that he could see God. Engine 8 had been there before us and they had taken consideralbe smoke. We all made it down the stairs while all hell was breaking loose up there. Fire was now showing from the front windows.

Bill and another guy from Eight's crew were on their way to the hospital with smoke inhalation. A few days later I went to visit him and explained that he had not seen God. What he did see was a statue of the Big Boss on the landing with a halo of very real fire around Him. I don't think Bill believed me.

As we made our exit we managed to save our hose line. We were now ordered to take the line down the tracks next to the loading dock. A ladder company threw a thirty-five foot ladder to the overhanging corrugated metal roof of an adjacent factory building.

The training instructors had drilled into us that if we were operating on a ladder we should remove our hose rope from our belt and hook it around our neck. This I did, and this saved four lives.

Because the roof was metal, the ladder was not dogged. I was the first one up and onto the roof and I scrambled to the wall. The roof had about a fifteen degree slope. There were three us, Bob, Fish Cakes and myself. The line was charged and we played water into the third and fourth floor windows. Sometimes the smoke was so heavy that we couldn't see the tracks below.

I had my back to a closed metal window shutter. We'd been in this location for about thirty minutes, long enough to begin to wonder if they were going to give us a break on the line. Then it happened—we were on a sheet of ice. I started to slide, slowly at first, like a film in slow motion. The hose was the first to go over the edge; we couldn't hold it. Captain Woolworth had just stepped off the ladder, I guess to tell us to get off the roof. I will never forget the look on his face. All four of us were sliding toward the edge. Instinctively I took the hose rope off my neck and put the steel ring over the hinge of the shutter. Bob Lowney was holding onto my boots. Fish Cakes was hold onto Bob's boots, and the captain was hanging onto Fish's boots. The ladder was long gone, crashing on the tracks below. Now I was stretched on my back—and my boots were coming off!

On the other end of the three-quarter inch hose rope is a hook. It was now making a hole in my glove and cutting into my hand. The faces of my wife, Peggy, and my boys came to my mind and I figured I was about to die. I remember starting to say a Hail Mary. To my left I could see Whitey Kivis of Ladder 2 also sliding off the roof in a sitting position. However, he was also doing something else. He was hitting the metal roof with his axe as he passed me.

Now I could feel the wet rusted roof under me. The sliding had stopped. A thin sheet of broken ice was sliding off the roof. No one had gone off. Captain Woolworth had stopped about a foot from the edge. A ladder was raised to us and we climbed down. I don't remember feeling the cold, only gratitude for the fact that we did not fall. It was then relief time and the night crew was there. We rode back to quarters on the hose wagon and the duty tour was finished.

A covering Boston engine company made fresh coffee for us, something of a tradition. When we covered at their station we did the same. We didn't discuss the close call. All I wanted to do was get home to my family. I did have trouble sleeping that night. The hole that the hook on the hose rope had made in my right hand kept reminding me of my slide down the roof. Even though I said nothing to Peggy, when she patted my shoulder I think she knew.

Some time later I met Whitey and thanked him. He said that he didn't remember seeing us...he was too busy trying to save his own life. Even today when I look at a hose rope...I remember.

Miracle on Market Street

It was a week before Christmas. At about ten o'clock we responded to a reported building fire on Market Street. On arrival we found we had a large six story, wood frame, multiple occupancy involved. Heavy smoke and fire were showing from the rear first floor windows and also on the upper floors. We were the second due engine and as we turned onto Clark Street, Acting Lieutenant Joe Maloney jumped from the pumper where he'd been riding, pointed at the third floor windows and calmly yelled, "We've got people up there!"

I pulled the hose wagon over to the side. We carried a wooden ladder on the side of the pump and the lieutenant was taking the ladder off. Looking up at the window, I saw three people hanging out. We threw the ladder up, Lieutenant Maloney climbed to the window. I footed the ladder. The first one down was an elderly lady; she had taken a lot of smoke and was almost fainting. The second one was a woman about thirty years old; she was yelling that her daughter was still up there. Joe went up again. I could see a young girl still in the window. As I watched, the fire blew out like a torch and the girl was gone.

Joe was at the window, but it was too late. He tried to feel inside, but it wasn't possible. The fire had started in the kitchen of the first floor. A woman was placing a glass, three gallon bottle of kerosene on the oil burner for fuel. She must have stumbled and broke the container on the stove. They found her body on the kitchen floor. The fire had blown out the kitchen door and right up the rear stairs. The kerosene was stored in fifty-five gallon drums in the basement, and the rear stairs' linoleum acted like a wick.

When the fire was knocked down, I went to the third floor bedroom where I had seen the girl. The room was black with soot and pretty well burnt-out. I knew her body had to be somewhere near the window, but I couldn't find it. A statue of the Blessed Virgin was on the bureau. Other firefighters were overhauling the room, pulling ceilings, looking for hidden fire. I didn't want the statue broken so I fished under the burned bed clothes and found a clean blanket. I wrapped the statue in the blanket and put it in a kitchen cabinet where I thought it would be safe.

When I looked down at the street from the bedroom window I saw a group of people. Lieutenant Maloney was there, as were the chief and a priest. Then, to my complete amazement, I saw the same young girl standing there talking. I knew it was the same girl—I could not forget that face.

She said that after Joe had taken her grandmother and then her mother down, the room got so hot she couldn't stand it. The statue of the Blessed Virgin glowed brightly and then spoke to her, saying, "Put your coat over your head and walk down the stairs." By this time the rear stairs were heavily involved in fire; it would not possible for anyone to walk down the back stairs. The front stairs were being used to advance lines and were heavily charged with smoke. No one passed the crews. The chief looked at the girl's shoes; there was only a small burn mark on one side.

To this day I have no idea how that girl was able to get out of that building.

A Subway Ride

We were standing in front of the apparatus doors one nice spring evening when a woman stopped her car and asked for directions to Harvard Square. I pointed to the overhead trolley wires and said, "Just follow the wire, ma'am, and they'll lead you right into the Square.

She followed my directions to the letter—right down the bus entrance ramp to the subway. We received a call later from the MBTA police requesting that we not tell anyone else to follow the overhead wires.

Another time a fellow asked us how to get to Antrim Street. "Simple, my friend," I replied, "take a right and go down two blocks."

Bill interrupted me and said, "Connie, you can't go that way, remember! The street's torn up. It'd be better if you went three blocks right, take a left and...."

"Good God, Bill, you got the poor guy going on a one way street in the wrong direction! Listen to me, mack, go straight ahead and cross the bridge and..."

Bill interrupted me again: "Mister, you listen to me..." then I looked at Bill and we both said, "Sorry, but you can't get there from here."

The fellow now had a completely blank look on his face as he said, "That's OK, I was supposed to pick up my wife, but I'm late anyway."

We now told him to relax, he wouldn't be late—Antrim Street was right at the end of our building.

Squires

During the early sixties the Cambridge Fire Department experienced a series of greater alarm fires. The second in the series was the Squires Complex. This meat packing plant had been in continuous operation for many, many years. The complex consisted of about ten brick and wood buildings, second class construction, located in a congested area of frame tenement houses in the East Cambridge section of the city. Shortly before the fire, the Squires Company ceased operation and the buildings were sold to a salvage/demolition company that was removing anything of value from the structures. The fire started in a seven story, mill-constructed factory in which bacon had been produced.

It was Easter Sunday and with the sun shining brightly it looked like it would be a beautiful day. As was our custom, we dressed the children in their Easter finery and headed for Grandmother's house in Boston's Lower Mills neighborhood for our Easter dinner. We left Grandma's house around 2:30 because I was scheduled to go into work at Engine 5 at 4:30. I was driving the hose wagon and would relieve my partner early so he too could enjoy Easter dinner with his family. As we were driving on the Expressway, Peggy pointed to a plume of black smoke rising up in front of us. At first it looked to me like the source of the smoke was in Charlestown or Somerville. As we drew nearer, however, it was quite apparent that it was, in fact, in Cambridge.

As we drove on Cambridge Street, just a block away, I could

see that the building was really involved, with heavy black smoke and flame showing from the upper floors. I took Peggy and the kids home, then left to report to Engine 5. "Be careful, hon!" Peg said to me as I left the house; she always did. I found a covering company in Engine 5's quarters. I got my helmet, rubber coat and boots, put them in the trunk of my car and drove down to the fire. It wouldn't be a good idea to park too close, so I found a spot two blocks away from the fire, which was on Gore Street. Engine 5's hose wagon was operating a deck gun on the Gore Street side of the complex.

When Lieutenant Magoon spotted me he said that we'd been ordered to take a line over a forty-five foot ladder and into the third floor. I took the pipe and Frank "Fish Cakes" Older was behind me, followed by the lieutenant. We weren't wearing masks. The heavy fire had been knocked down by the guns and the smoke conditions weren't really that bad. We were on a good solid floor. This was a meat packing plant and was built to take a lot of weight. Getting real low, we started to advance the line straight ahead. Ahead of me I saw a light. It was a chief officer, and he told us that all the fire was extinguished on that floor and he would show us the stairs leading to the floor above.

They pulled in more line for us and we followed him up the stairs to the fourth floor. The smoke still wasn't too bad; the building was wide open and most of the windows had been removed. The fourth floor was rolling. There was heavy fire as far as I could see. Scavengers had gotten into the floors and had been using burning torches to get at copper and brass in the walls. This floor contained huge walk-in freezers covered with varnished wainscoting. Years ago they used sawdust as insulation and this too was burning.

About this time someone started tugging on our hose line. I was lying on the floor at the head of the stairs, waiting for the line to be charged. The fire ahead of us was really building. Tongues of flame were now lapping over my head and the sound roared like a freight train. Then I heard someone yelling, "Get out! Get out quick!" It was time to leave. Great beams of wood began to fall from the ceiling ahead of me and tumbling down the stairs. The building was coming apart.

I held tight to the nozzle as we backed down the stairs.

Conditions on this floor, the third floor, had deteriorated. Heavy, choking smoke with little visibility—now the smoke had us gasping for breath. The line was being pulled back. We are trained to stay with the line because it will lead you out and I held tight to the pipe. Now I could see the outline of the window through which we entered and the line was moving faster now and then we were at the window. I took one last look back and saw that the fire was now spreading across the entire ceiling. I threw the pipe over my shoulder, stepped out the window and descended the ladder. We would never get back into that building.

It was now time for an exterior attack. The portable deck gun was removed from the deck of the hose wagon and three 2½ inch lines were run into it. Fish Cakes, Don and I were on the gun. Heavy fire was now pouring from every single window of the third and fourth floors. The flag pole fell from the upper floors and landed across our lines; the red hot metal began to burn the hose. Don and I tried to move the pole, but it was too heavy. Now chunks of wall were falling around us and red hot bricks cascaded like stone confetti. I heard someone yelling to drag the gun back away from the falling wall. We attempted to do this. My left leg was between the legs of the gun. A large section of the wall crashed down onto the street very close to us. Everyone ran and the gun began sliding along the street. A metal leg has slid up my boot and I am trapped under; I am in deep trouble and I know it. The gun is crushing my leg and has me pinned to the street. The whole damn wall was starting to come down on top of me and I kept yelling like a banshee for help. Lieutenant Magoon was the first back, then Don, Fish Cakes and Fitzy. They manage to free me and we all ran up Marion Street like Satan himself was chasing after us. We ran by Leo McDugal who was trying to get Five's pump disconnected from the hydrant at the corner of Gore and Marion Streets.

All hell was breaking loose behind us. The entire front wall of the seven story building collapsed in a ground shaking crash. The concussion blew Lt. Magoon's rubber coat over his head. As I hobbled along behind him it looked to me as if his head had been blown off. He stumbled and fell. The force of the collapse knocked the rest of us down and we rolled up Marion Street. My leg hurt like hell but I still could run.

We didn't stop until we hit Cambridge Street. It was mass confusion. How many firefighters were trapped under the bricks? The heat radiated from the main fire and the buildings across the street now began to burn. The telephone poles were on fire and power lines on the street were aflame.

A chief ordered us to enter the lard factory and check for open windows. This was a six story brick building similar in construction to and directly across the street from the one that had just collapsed. When Fitzy and I reached the top floor we found that the window frames facing the fire were starting to burn. Fitzy walked off and came back with a soda and acid extinguisher. We wet down as many windows as we could before the extinguisher emptied.

Don and Lt. Magoon were doing the same thing below us on the fifth floor. It started to get real smoky and Fitzy suggested that we better get the hell out. We made our way down the rear stairs to the fourth floor where we discovered that fire had already entered and was cutting us off. We knew mayhem was down below us. We yelled for a ladder, but no one was paying much attention to us. Lt. Magoon yelled down the hall that we could get out another window and jump to an adjoining roof. This we did, with my bad leg and all. From there we went down a fire escape to the rear yard.

A ladder truck was trapped in the rear yard. The debris from the wall collapse made it impossible for the truck to get back out to Gore Street. Firefighters, civilians and police were trying to tear down a chain link fence so the ladder truck could escape up Marion Street. Finally they knocked the fence down, but there was a difference in grade of about one foot.

The driver backed up the ladder truck as far as possible for a running start. At full throttle he hit the grade change and the cab jumped over, then the rear wheels hit and the tillerman flew into the air but he was able to hang on. They made it—the truck drove up Marion Street and out of danger.

All the buildings across the street from the main fire were now seriously exposed. Two were already burning, the lard factory and a storage garage. A desperate effort was now underway to relocate hose lines in order to play water on the exposures. Charged lines were scarce at this point. New lines had to run from available water supply on Cambridge Street.

The fire was now well past a general alarm. Mutual aid apparatus from as far away as Quincy were now arriving. We found a one and a half inch hose that had some water in it; Fitzy and I got up on the roof of a garage and tried to wet down the side of an exposed structure. Bob Correll was down in the yard with another hose. He had less water pressure than we had, but he was able to wet us down; we would catch the water from his hose and fill our helmets; the splashing water over our heads helped a little. The intense heat turned all hose streams to steam and the water was not reaching the fire. We'd already turned our helmets around so that the brims would act as shields. Aluminum helmets are noted for their heat reflection. Our ears were badly burned.

By this time four of five buildings of the complex were involved. Conditions at the rear were slightly better because there was more room to maneuver. A Boston Engine company lugged a two and a half inch hose up to the roof and the officer told us to go and take a break. Up on Cambridge Street, Fitzy and I sat down in a doorway. When he asked how my leg was I shook my head and said, "It hurts like a bastard but I guess it's OK." I had lost some skin on my shin bone. I noticed a rivulet of blood running down Fitzy's neck from the burns on his ears. When I mentioned it to him, he started to laugh, finally saying, "Obie, I thought you were wearing red ear rings!"

About twenty guys were sitting or lying on the sidewalk, some suffering from heat exhaustion and smoke inhalation, others from fatigue. A nurse moved among them administering oxygen and checking for other injuries. Don arrived and told us he knew where we ccould get a cup of coffee. We located a Red Cross disaster wagon up the street. They gave us a cup of coffee and some crackers. My God did that coffee and those crackers taste good! Our faces were black and we all had exposure burns.

The fire had crowned, that is passed its most severe intensity, and was starting to show signs of control. Gore Street was covered with piles of hot brick; the tip of the deck gun that I was trapped under was sticking out of three feet of bricks. All the hose we were using was buried under the brick. Companies were moving into the exposed buildings and extinguishing hot spots.

Deputy Chief Levin told us to go back to quarters and change our clothes; we were soaked to the skin. Thank God it was a warm day and there was no ice involved. When I found my car I also found that it had been wrecked. As I stood there looking at my automobile, a Somerville police officer informed me that a fire engine had hit it. It wasn't that it was a new car, but it was the only car I owned. It too was a casualty of the fire. A tow truck took it away and I hitched a ride back to the firehouse.

I called home to let Peg know that I was OK. I didn't tell her about the car; that would keep for later. It was always hard for her to be at home hearing the news flashes about men injured, not knowing if I was one of them. I am sure that every time the phone rang her heart would leap a bit. Sometimes she would get a call informing her that I was injured, but I always tried to avoid this. When I walked into the house with a bandage, she would look at me and say, "What happened, hon? Are you OK?"

I returned to the Squire Complex and spent the night there. The falling wall had also broken the large gas main on Gore Street; fire broke out again in the basement of the office building during the night, and we had a very difficult time getting at it. The two story wood frame structure had partially collapsed and the fire was burning along the ceiling. In order to get at it we had to crawl into the cellar. Two Somerville firefighters were missing and supposed to be in that area. We found a hose line going down a corridor and then ending due to the collapse. We checked the marking on the hose; it was a Somerville line. If there was anyone on the nozzle, they could be down there with the rest of the line. The cellar was so flooded that the water was over our heads.

We were discussing the possibility of getting a small boat and searching the cellar when it was reported to us that the men had been accounted for and were OK. We found another way into the cellar and went in. There were lots of creaking timbers down there—and two more stories of tilted building above us. We hit as much fire as we could then made a hasty exit. The folks running the show decided to allow the fire to burn out—it was just too dangerous for firefighters to conduct any further fire operations.

When the sun finally rose, let me tell you, I was one tired puppy. We were dismissed by the day crew and I bummed a ride home. On the way we saw fire and smoke ahead of us in North Cambridge. It was a restaurant at Fresh Pond Circle. I went home, kissed my wife, hugged my kids, and was asleep when my head hit the pillow.

Cambridge ladderwork in the early 50s.
(Photo courtesy of Dan Murphy)

The face says it all—a rookie's anticipation of adventure!

Rescues over ladders in a furniture store fire. Note the lack of masks.
(Photo courtesy of Calvin Campbell)

Carstine's Coal Yard—one of the Easter Sunday fires.
(Photo by Joseph Eldridge)

Another shot of Carstine's.
(Photo courtesy of Gerry Mahoney)

Spectators wore their Easter best to watch Cartsine's.
(Photo by Joseph Eldridge)

Fire extending to exposures on Cogswell Avenue.
(Photo by Joseph Eldridge)

The bell tower fire at Harvard's Memorial Hall. It was a tough climb to the roof.
(Photo courtesy of Gerry Mahoney.)

We turned our helmets against the heat at the New England Brick Yard fire. The
author is on the pipe in this photo by Joe Eldridge.

The fire has just blown out the window of this Market Street fire—where the miracle occured. (Photo courtesy of William Ramskiwiz)

The International Alley Cat's short wheel-base let it turn around on a dime or down a narrow Cambridge street. (Photo by Ed Fowler)

Cambridge Rescue crew and piece from the early 70s.
(Photo courtesy of Ed Fowler)

Engine 7 in 1972. Capt. Connie O'Brien is on the left.

Deputy Chief Kevin Fitzgerald stands before a working Maxim pumper.
(Photo by John Hathaway)

Getting ready to move in from the alley.
(Photo by Dan Turner)

Things are better now than in the old days—and easier on the lungs.
(Photo by Dan Turner)

Red hot and first in. Nobrega's was a huge fabric/curtain/linens store,
which made for extremely smokey conditions. (Photo by Dan Turner)

Inside and moving forward.
(Photo by Dan Turner)

Ladderwork in the 90s.
(Photo by Dan Turner)

The sale will probably be bigger than they'd planned!
(Photo by Dan Turner)

Sunday morning special. The fire started in the rear kitchen of the first floor then raced up the back stairs to the third floor. (Photo by John Hathaway)

Multi-story/multi-unit/multi-purpose—it still burns.
(Photo by Bill Noonan)

Chief of Dept. Kevin Fitzgerald and Deputy Chief Connie O'Brien stand before a 1935 Seagrave pumper. Dan Maloney is behind the wheel. (Photo by Ed Fowler)

To those who have gone before. (Photo by Dan Turner)

Part Two

Sock in the Jaw

After the great Squires meat packing fire, I was appointed acting lieutenant at Engine Company 5 with a float to Ladder 2 on Portland Street for a short time. This company is located near the city line between Cambridge and Somerville. Consequently, we answered many line boxes, that is responding to boxes out of the city. A box alarm for a pull box or a call for a fire in either city would receive the response of three engine companies and two ladder companies.

One morning we responded to a line box alarm in Somerville for a structure fire. We were first to arrive at the scene. There was heavy smoke showing from a two and a half story frame occupied dwelling with fire visible in the cellar. As I got off the pump, a civilian grabbed me and shouted that a girl was trapped on the second floor and a police officer had gone up to get her out. After giving a radio report to Cambridge Fire Alarm, who then relayed the information to the Somerville Fire Department, I entered the first floor hallway.

The police officer was falling down the stairs and coughing badly. He told me that he was able to get as far as the second floor landing but then the smoke was too much. Donning my all-service mask, I reached the second floor. As I crawled down the hallway I heard a faint moan. I found a very large woman slumped over the couch. As I reached for her she jumped at me and we both started rolling on the floor. I pleaded with her to stop and leave the building with me—but to no avail. She was trying to pull off my mask. I could see the fire in the rear of the apartment starting to enter the room along the ceiling; I decided there was no time left for diplomacy. I hit the woman in the face once and she stopped struggling with me.

Using my legs as a brace against the couch, I was able to drag her on her back toward the door. Some other guys were in the hall and removed her from the building. We proceeded to assist in extinguishing the fire, and we were dismissed by the Somerville chief.

The next day I was sitting at the patrol desk when Deputy Chief O'Mally came in to pick up the morning reports. He told me that the woman I'd hit was the sister of a firefighter stationed at Cambridge Engine 9. Furthermore, the deputy added, I had broken her jaw and the guy was on his way down to Engine 5 to break my head.

As I tried to explain the circumstances surrounding my hitting the woman, the deputy said, "Lieutenant, I am just telling you what I've heard. You will have to deal with the matter yourself." He left quarters and I just sat at the patrol desk contemplating my fate. I knew the man who was coming to pummel me. He was bigger than I. He was also a prize fighter. I truly didn't know what to do—cut and run or stand and try to explain. As I sat there the door opened and there he was, six feet tall and built like a Seagrave pumper. Holding up my hand and pleading for calm, I said, "Spike, let me explain, please...." He put both his arms around me, squeezed tight, then started crying and saying, "Thank you, Connie, thank you!" over and over. I started crying too; of course, my tears were those of relief and joy because Spike was not going to make a punching bag of me.

When we quieted down he explained over a cup of coffee that he hadn't come to pummel me. His sister was severely retarded and living with family friends in the building that burned. Furthermore, she was not in the hospital, nor did she have a broken jaw. Spike just wanted to thank me for saving his sister's life. What a nice guy!

Deputy Chief O'Mally was a rogue and having some fun with me. Spike kept me informed on how his sister was doing and we remained good friends. About three years after this incident, Spike was severely injured in a fall from a roof at a fire in North Cambridge; he retired with a disability pension.

The Boys on the Train

My next assignment as a fire lieutenant was floating officer between Engine 9 and Engine 4, both located in North Cambridge. This meant that I had two of everything—two captains over me; two crews to work with; two different lockers; two shields for my helmet. You might say that I lived out of a bag. Sometimes I would get confused driving up Massachusetts Avenue; I would have to stop and think, "Where the hell am I supposed to be working today?" A few times I actually drove into the rear of a station and parked my car before I realized I was at the wrong firehouse. Still, although being a float was generally considered an undesirable assignment, and even though it did have some inconveniences, I thought it was a great way to learn the district, work with different guys, and get more varied experience as an officer.

At about three o'clock one morning we received an alarm for a building fire on Richdale Avenue. A very heavy snowstorm was just ending. Fire Alarm was now telling the responding deputy chief that they were receiving calls for a fire in the Allied Storage warehouse. This was a large four story brick warehouse located along the Boston and Maine railroad tracks. The tracks run north and south toward Boston. The building faces on Richdale Ave. and had a long loading dock in the rear. Not unlike many of this type of storage building, the Allied Storage warehouse had few windows. Firefighting in this type of structure is often very difficult due the inability of placing hose streams.

As we passed over the bridge from Massachusetts Ave. on to Upland Road, I could see heavy fire up the tracks in the direction of the warehouse. The whole damn area was glowing orange. I didn't hesitate and notified Fire Alarm: "Engine 4 to Fire Alarm." "Answering Engine 4." "On the orders of Lieutenant O'Brien, Engine Four, box 7134 is a working fire—I repeat, a working fire!"

We laid a big line and located the pump at the hydrant in preparation for a hard fight. The other responding companies started arriving and everyone started looking for the big fire. The only trouble was that there was nothing but complete darkness up the track. Deputy Chief Rogan arrived and wanted to know where all the fire was. I explained what I'd seen and he replied, "Where the *hell* is the fire, Lieutenant? Go find the fire!"

Mike Handier had slid down the snow bank to the tracks and was calling me down. Up the tracks about fifty yards was some kind of train. We also noticed a heavy smell of diesel in the air. As I approached the train I could see men standing by the engine looking like the mouse that had swallowed the cat. I asked the little guy smoking the pipe what the hell was going on. In a fine, soft Irish accent he replied, "Sure now, we're only melting the snow back from the switches."

It turned out that they had caused a commotion in every town they'd passed through. The deputy dismissed all the apparatus, then told me in no uncertain terms that the next time I was to look before I acted.

To a Chief

I was not on duty when Fitzy went through the roof. When I reported for work the next morning they told me that there had been a three bagger at the motel on Route 2. Fitzy and I had worked together at Engine 5 and he was now the captain of Rescue One. The fire was in a two and three story motel that was attached to a car wash. It had started somewhere within the motel and when our units arrived at three o'clock in the morning, people were making a hasty exit. These types of occupancies, fortunately, do have notification systems and sprinklers. Rescue One was on the roof of the car wash. Very heavy smoke conditions existed. As they groped across towards the windows of the motel, Fitzy fell through the roof. When they got to him, he was severely injured. He had landed on his back and his air tank caused internal injuries. He also suffered injuries to his face and left eye.

Whether or not Fitzy would make it was touch and go for a couple of days. I visited him at the Cambridge Hospital and he was really hurting. He couldn't talk, but he did give me a wink. Fitzy is a former Marine and a tough guy. I owe my life to him. He was one of the three guys who pulled me from under the deluge gun at the Squire's fire.

Fitzy was finally released from the hospital and was recuperating from home. One night the union was having a special meeting on an issue that I can't now remember. The meeting was held in the second floor hall of the VFW Post in North Cambridge. And there Fitzy stood, at the foot of the stairs, ready to attend the meeting. We were all amazed. Two or three of the guys hustled down the stairs to carry him up, but he would have none of it. Waving his cane, he yelled, "Stand back, you jerks! I'm OK."

Encouraging words flew as Fitzy used the cane and the banister. He had a look of complete determination on his face. Finally he reached the top of the landing. I will never forget the ovation he received—every member there was clapping.

Fitzy went on to become the Chief of the Cambridge Fire Department. To this day he continues to show the same leadership and determination he demonstrated that night.

The Spinning Grill

We kept a round charcoal grill on the flat roof of headquarters. Sometimes the guys from Engine 1, Ladder 1 and the Rescue Company would pitch in and one of the guys would buy some really fine steaks, then we'd get together on the roof on a Sunday at noon for a cookout. One guy would stop at a bakery for rolls; another guy would bring in a huge bowl of his wife's potato salad; and I will always remember the wonderful taste of those homemade chocolate cookies.

There we'd be, all standing around the circular grill, cooking our own piece steak. John Dimmings would say to me, "Hey, Loot, is that smoke in the sky?" When I turned to look he would spin the grill and start poking my steak. I guess it looked juicier than his and he wanted it. Sometimes that grill would spin like a top as everyone tried to get a better looking cut of meat. Usually the Rescue would get a call and by the time they'd get back, only the poorest and sickest pieces remained.

I remember another day when John Dimmings reported for duty without having any supper. We were all sitting at the kitchen table having a cup of coffee and John began rummaging through the refrigerator. Before too long he found a full dinner in a brown bag. When he held up the bag and asked, "Anyone belong to this?" One of the Rescue guys replied that it had been left by the guy he'd relieved. He also said the fellow hadn't felt well and had left the dinner bag there.

That was all John needed to hear. He gobbled it up and for a short time I thought we would lose the plate. Just as he finished,

Chief Rollins entered the kitchen and started to search the refrigerator. I could hear him grumbling about a dinner that should be in there. One by one we left the kitchen before the fireworks started.

John was looking a little sick. Maybe it was due to eating too fast. Maybe it was due to bad timing. But the chief was now confronting John, nose to nose: "Did you eat my fucken dinner, Dimmings?" John's mouth opened but no words came out. Now the chief was screaming: "You asshole! Did you eat my baked ham dinner that Millie made for me?" John's face was becoming gray. I heard something that sounded like *Ba-ba-ummm-aarrrr*. It was hard to make out, but I figured John had shit his pants.

The chief called for his aide and off they roared to get him some dinner. Most of the guys were sprawled on the floor of the TV room, laughing so hard they looked like they were in pain. John was in the bathroom. I don't think he ever raided the fridge again.

The Accelerator

The Fourth of July celebrations usually quieted down after about one in the morning on the fifth of July. Before that we would be getting a series of false alarms downtown in Division 1. It had been a muggy night, the kind of sticky, clinging night when it is hard to get to sleep, so most of us were awake when the explosion caused all the doors in headquarters to go up. The whole building shook and everyone started to yell, "What the hell was that!"

Now the tone was signaling a box for the Dewy Almy Chemical Plant; the chief in Division 2 and Rescue responded. Since this box was located way up in North Cambridge, we realized it must have been quite an explosion for us to feel and hear it down here at headquarters. Another tone and then: "Box 6724 is being struck for an explosion in the atomic reactor at Oxford and Wendell Streets." Everyone goes, Ladder 1, Engine 1, and the other division chief.

"Fire Alarm calling C 2."

"Answering."

"C 2, we have another box in for Dewy Almy and now we are receiving calls that the Harvard Accelerator has exploded."

"Message received from C 2." Ladder 1 was in front us as we raced up Oxford Street and I could see the tillerman pointing to the sky and then I could see it over the roofs of the buildings—the whole damn sky was red and a gigantic plume of jet black smoke was moving quickly upward.

We took a hydrant on Oxford Street because there was a

chance that the private mains within Harvard's property had been destroyed by the explosion. Of course, I had to worry that the lay would not be too long, that we'd have enough hose to reach the building. God Almighty what a sight awaited us. The building was a round shaped structure approximately three hundred feet in circumference, about forty feet high, and constructed entirely of concrete and steel. The structure's roof was designed and built with the knowledge that an explosion was a real possibility. There were also at least four levels underground, and a two lane ramp led to various underground loading docks.

As we approached the building, Chief O'Connell held up his hand to us and said, "Nobody goes near this until we can check for radiation hazard." We held back and waited as the chief radioed Fire Alarm to strike a second alarm; he also ordered the Rescue to respond to the scene as quickly as possible.

Harvard University police officers advised us that some type of experimental procedure had been conducted below but they did not know very much about what had happened. We always had an excellent working relationship with them and we waited for the radiation tests. Rescue arrived and when their examination of the area for possible radiation came back negative, the chief turned to me and said, "Lieutenant, advance your line down the ramp and look for possible survivors. And be careful!" I assured the chief that I certainly intended to be just that.

A large trailer truck parked at the foot of the ramp made it difficult to advance a line. As we passed the truck cab, Speedy grabbed a look to see if there was a driver inside, but it was empty. We crawled down the ramp and the smoke was so thick that visibility was zero, the heat was terrific, and I could see heavy flame ahead through the smoke. I was now worried about the contents of that trailer truck.

When the line was charged and we started to hit the fire, we were doing little actual good. The heat was getting much worse and someone was yelling down the ramp, "Engine 1! Engine 1! Back out now!" Staying with the hose, we kept the pipe over our heads. The water came back down on us boiling hot as we crawled back toward the ramp opening.

We were now back outside. By now we had gone to four alarms with special calls for air cylinders and another Rescue Company. Flames were shooting at least one hundred feet into the air. Fortunately, due to its location, the exposure problem was minimal. A team of scientists from both Harvard and MIT were now at the scene. They informed the chief that when the explosion occurred, at least four men were in the underground control gallery. These men would be behind massive shields of lead and could survive the blast.

Chief O'Connell assigned a team of ten men consisting of the Rescue and an engine company to descend to the gallery and search for survivors. They were advised that there was an entrance to the bunker behind the parking lot on Prentiss Street. Led by Lieutenant Walter Loring from the Rescue Company, the firefighters started down the bunker stairs, each man carrying various pieces of equipment—rope, forcible entry tools, bright lights, spare air cylinders, portable radio equipment. Heavy black smoke poured out the already opened bunker door. The heat was not that intense. Following the railing of the cement stairs, the crew advanced down into the darkness and heat below. They'd tied a lifeline to the bumper of the truck and taken it along to show the way out. The engine crew advanced a cover line in case the team encountered any fire. When Walter came to the end of the stairs, he started crawling ahead on what felt like a corridor. Now there was terrific heat. Visibility was zero and they could hear the sounds of small explosions ahead of them. Suddenly Water felt someone grab his coat. It was a man's hand! The rescue team searched in the blackness and heat and found two more victims.

Everyone reached the surface safely. The men had been horribly burned; their skin hanging off them. They were practically naked. Medical help was waiting and they were taken to the burn center of the Mass. General Hospital. Two of the rescued men later died in the hospital of their burns. The chief ordered an exterior attack and we set up heavy stream appliances to surround the site. For the remainder of the night, tons of water were poured on the fire. Most of the fire had darkened down by daybreak. A forty-five foot ladder was placed against the side of the structure and we were ordered to operate a two and a half inch line from the ladder. Looking down inside I could see the damage the explosion had caused. The solid concrete roof had been moved about three feet, twisted steel girders look like pretzels, and here and there gas cylinders were burning as they vented. It was a scene of utter devastation.

As relief time approached the day shift began showing up at the scene. I understand that lines were later advanced inside to cover emergency crews as they attempted to shut down various gas lines. The search team found the body of the fourth victim in the gallery area; he had been burned to death where he stood.

Back at the station the covering companies had the hot coffee waiting for us and some good-hearted soul had stopped at a bakery. I had a lovely cup of coffee and a doughnut, cleaned up and headed for my home and family, happy to be starting three days off.

Bicycle Inspection

While I was stationed at headquarters near Harvard Square, bicycles were registered and issued a number plate. This was necessary because Cambridge is a college city with many bicycles on the streets. Although it had nothing to do with the Cambridge Fire Department, for some reason bicycle registration was conducted upstairs on the second floor of the Cambridge Fire Department headquarters.

John Dimmings was a real clown assigned to Engine One. One day he was sitting at the patrol desk and a young guy came in looking to have his bike inspected and registered. The apparatus floor had just been washed and was still wet. John told the guy that he'd take good care of him. He next told the bike owner to go back to the apparatus door, get on the bike and peddle as fast as he could until John told him to apply the brakes. The fellow did as he was told and the bike was going top speed when John yelled, *"Brakes!"*

As I said, the floor was wet and there was a slick of oil on it. The brakes were fine, John later said, but the bicyclist skidded across the floor and out the rear door and was gone. About fifteen minutes later he came back and wanted to know if his bike passed the test. He had a bandage on his chin and his clothes were quite torn. Firefighter Dimmings was severely reprimanded for his action and told not to conduct any additional inspections.

A week or so later a student came into quarters looking to have his bike inspected. The man on the floor patrol—who just happened to be our good friend, John—sent the young man to the second floor, telling him to "Just carry the bike up." Naturally, as the student and his bike went up the stairs everyone else was forced against the walls of the stairs. This time the chief had a few choice words to say to our house clown.

John knew Engine 1's district very, very well. One day when were out conducting in-service inspections, an alarm can in for a building fire on Athens Street. For the life of me I could not think of where the street was. I asked John and he said the he'd never heard of it. I stuck my head into the street directory and went to work. As I feverishly thumbed through the directory, the engine raced down the street. John poked me in the ribs and said, "Here we are, Lieutenant." He'd known where Athens Street was all along. He simply enjoyed seeing his lieutenant flustered.

Sometimes, of course, life is the prankster...even for our firehouse clown.

Friday was trash day on the street. One Friday afternoon John decided to clean out the inside of his car, so he removed the seats and placed them against some rubbish barrels. We had an alarm of fire which turned out to be false. When John went back out to his car after we returned from the run, the rubbish had been picked up and his seats were on the way to the dump. I gave him permission to go looking for his car seats. He stopped at least five garbage trucks and looked inside, but to no avail. That night, they told me, he was at the dump with a flashlight searching for his seats. He never found them, and he used milk cases for as long as he kept that car.

A Flying Rope

We responded to a fire in a construction site in Harvard Square. There had been an explosion due to an incident involving propane gas, and when we arrived there was heavy fire on the fourth and fifth floors of the structure. The standpipe in the building was not hooked up so we had to provide water from the street. I had a rookie assigned to the company, and I told him to get a hauling line and follow me. When we reached the third floor I found a guy badly burned and the Rescue crew removed him.

It was open construction at that point, no walls at all. We made our way to the edge. Since I intended to haul up a hose, I told my rookie to throw the hauling line down to the street. So he did. Yes, I meant for him to tie off the line to the rail first. The untied line, still coiled, flew through the air and landed—naturally— on the roof of a chief's car who had just arrived at the scene.

Needless to say I was upset. The chief was upset, but somehow the fire was successfully extinguished. The rookie and I had a little training session later in the day and I do think he now has the right idea.

The Red Lady on Green Street

The fire was roaring in a three story duplex on Green Street, and we responded on the third alarm. When I reported to the chief at the front of the building, he ordered me to take my crew and advance a line up the rear stairs to the second floor. There was very heavy smoke in the rear hall. When we reached the kitchen, I couldn't see any fire, only the thick smoke. I crawled around and found a narrow stairway leading up to an attic space. Figuring it unlikely that anyone had been up there, I still had to be sure, so I told the guys to cover me with the line while I took a look.

When I reached the top of the stairs there was some visibility. It was a hallway that led toward the front and rear. A ladderman was coming through the rear window. I could see the top of his helmet painted red. He met me in the hall and I told him to search the rear rooms; I moved down the hall toward the front.

There was a room on my right. The door was open. In the corner of the far side of the room was a bed up against the wall, and in the bed was a naked young girl. She was in a sitting position against the wall. Just over her head was a hole that was cut by a truck company. The laths and plaster were all over her and the bed.

My boys on the line were yelling that the fire was breaking out in the kitchen below and it was time to back down. I reached over the bed and pulled the girl toward me. She was as red as a lobster. Her eyes were partly open and mucus was hanging from her nose. She was in bad shape.

I yelled through my facepiece that I had found someone. By this time we could feel the heat from downstairs and visibility was almost zero. With the help of the truckie in the hall I was able to get the girl to the head of the stairs; I took off my mask, opened the emergency by-pass and pressed it against her face. It was too late—there was heavy fire below and my ears were starting to burn. We dragged her to the rear window through which the ladderman had entered. Fortunately, the ladder was still there.

The truckie got out on the ladder and I passed the girl to him. The fire was right behind me. We got out of there none too soon. I knew that my crew would be worried about me so I went around and let them know that we got out OK. The fire now had a good hold on the attic and roof. Looking back up there I hoped that no other people were in the attic which was now a raging sea of flame.

Eventually, of course, the fire was extinguished; no one else was found. Two days later I was ordered to report to headquarters to see the division chief. Apparently the girl I found nearly died from carbon monoxide poisoning; that was the reason she was so red. The chief wanted to know the circumstances of my finding her. After I explained the whole incident to the chief he said, "Lieutenant, there have been some serious charges made against you."

"Who's making the charges, Chief?" I asked.

"The young lady told her father that the firemen who found her took all her clothes off."

This was a stunning bit of information. The chief wanted a full investigation into the matter. I just shook my head in disbelief. He then told me to write a full report; the truckie, a fellow from Ladder 4, also had to file a report.

About a week later I was again told to report to headquarters. This time things were different. We were told the following story by the girl's father: there'd been a pot party going on in the building, and the girl and her boyfriend went up to the attic bedroom to engage in a little belly-bumping. They didn't notice that the fire had broken out because they were a little involved, and then they found themselves trapped. The brave lad apparently bailed out a window; a friend of mine who was a photographer for one of the area's large newspapers showed me a photo of the bare assed bucko sliding down a drain pipe. He'd just bailed out and left the girl there.

The father extended his hand and apologized for any inconvenience he might have caused me, explaining that his daughter was a student in a large local college and had got mixed up with the SDS, Students for a Democratic Society. She concocted the story so daddy wouldn't discover that she was no longer his sexually innocent little girl. As I shook the man's hand I told him that he should really go down to Ladder 3 and thank the man who put the hole in the roof directly over the girl's head that saved her life. I don't know if he ever did.

Follow the Line

The third came in real quick. We usually covered on the second alarm for a fire so far north, but a still alarm for a gas dryer had us down on Magazine Street, a few blocks from our station. The minute we cleared the still, Fire Alarm called us on the radio and ordered the company to respond directly to the fire.

As we headed up Massachusetts Avenue we could see the loom up. Heavy black smoke was showing from four miles ahead. Fortunately, traffic was not too bad at three in the afternoon of a workday. Just as we approached, I received radio orders to report to Deputy Chief Muligan in front of the fire building.

He was there waiting for us. It was an old, four story, second class Odd Fellows Hall. The fire had started somewhere in the rear and was spreading upward. "Lieutenant," ordered the chief, "stretch a two and a half inch line to the fourth floor and check for extension of fire in the rear of the auditorium."

We donned our self-contained breath apparatus. Charlie Butterworth and I lightened up on the line. The front stairs were wide and clear and we had no problems making the fourth floor. As we passed the third floor landing, the smoke was starting to get heavy and I noted that two companies were advancing lines down the hallways. Smoke was hanging two feet off the floor. We were, I think, the first company to reach the fourth floor level. Keeping low, we dragged the dry line down the corridor toward the auditorium. I was behind the pipeman and Charlie was behind me. Visibility in the big hall was pretty good. We had gone about fifty feet when I saw the glow of fire behind the stage curtain. Then I heard a crashing sound and I looked up at the high ceiling and saw large pieces of plaster falling and heavy fire where the plaster had just been. The smoke was now down to the floor and I couldn't see my hand in front of me. A piece of the ceiling hit me on my helmet, stunning me. I laid on my back and tried to clear my head and that must have been when I lost the hose.

Never leave the hose was a maxim that had been hammered into us since drill school. The hose will show you the way out. However, when the plaster fell on top of me and I fell, Joe and Charlie must have moved further to my left. All hell was now breaking loose as large pieces of plaster rained down. I had lost my hand light, probably when I fell. The air regulator in my mask was really clicking. My air supply was good for thirty minutes of normal breathing, but I was using air fast. The line was gone and I completely lost my sense of direction. *"Joe!...Charlie!"* No answer. There I was, sitting on the floor of an auditorium with the ceiling falling. I looked to my right and saw the smoke become lighter for a moment. I stumbled again, over another chair. This time I landed on my hands and knees and was able to maintain the direction of the change in smoke color. With both hands in front of me I continued groping forward. We weren't equipped with portable radios at this time. I could feel the panic building in me and the thought of the possibility of dying was becoming very real to me and I began to pray *Hail, Mary, full of grace*...and on I stumbled, I hoped in the right direction, as beams smashed down behind me and just when I was convinced that this was the end, that I was going to die, my outstretched hand felt a wall.

It was a door. Now I could feel the panic bar, a type of emergency door release used in places of assembly. This was my last shot and I knew it. I pushed the door open and I was out on a fire escape. The alarm bell on my now empty air cylinder was ringing.

The roof was now collapsing. Bill Sweeney of Ladder 4 was there. He asked me where the hell I'd come from. He told me that he opened the door for a moment but there was no line on the fire escape so he closed the door to prevent a backdraft that would have intensified the fire. This was the change in smoke color that I saw. It had saved my life.

He started to pull me down the fire escape and I was yelling that we had to go back in because two more men were in there. I remember him saying that it was too late. My hands trembled as I pulled off my mask. The feeling in my stomach was indescribable. Now I was on the street. The roof had burned off and companies were assuming defensive positions and going into heavy stream appliances. Flames were fifty feet in the air.

I will never forget the feeling that devoured me as I approached the command post to report the loss of my men. I should be in there with them. The cold sweat was running down my back. Two men were talking to the chief of department; I realized that the two men were Charlie and Joe. They had just reported my death. Joe saw me first. The tears were streaming down his face as he ran toward me. Charlie just stood there with an amazed look on his face. We embraced each other, only briefly because there was much work to do to contain this fire.

Later Joe and Charlie told me over a cup of coffee that they had moved to the left and then became aware that I was no longer with them on the line. They yelled for me but the crashing plaster forced them to move further away. Another engine company had made their way up a rear side stairway and come across Joe and Charlie. They abandoned the hose line and they all made it down the rear stairs.

This is, I think, why firefighters are so close. At some time during a career you find yourself in a situation when you feel that there is a good chance you won't make it out. We did make it, but I still think that we were sheltered by angels' wings and a voice saying, "Not this time...not this time."

When I got home that night I gave my wife and my kids extra strong hugs.

Fleas In My Seat

Wednesday was inspection day. Companies would go out either in the morning or afternoon; you were out of normal service during this time. Ladder 2's district was highly commercial with lumber yards, coal yards and factories, but the district did have a residential area consisting primarily of tenements. Inspections were conducted once a week, and every day except Sunday during Fire Prevention Week. It took approximately three years to complete the circuit.

We parked on Gore Street and I assigned each of my four men dwellings to inspect. We maintained a card system and when the inspection was made, the date and condition of the property were noted on the card. We pointed out any fire hazards or other conditions that needed attention to the property owner or building superintendent.

Dink Muller, my tillerman, came out of a cellar and told me that he had encountered a dead cat and was now infested with fleas. He was in really bad shape, scratching and squirming around. I told him we would return to quarters and he could take a bath. As soon as we pulled up at the front doors, Dink jumped down from the tiller seat. Tim Lonavin was the spare tillerman, so I told him to jump up. We have a buzzer signal system that allows the tillerman to tell the driver that he is in position and ready to roll. We did not get any signal. We waited some more...still no signal. Finally, I walked back and there was Timmy intently studying the tiller seat and cushion.

"What's the trouble, Timmy?" I asked.

"Lieutenant, there are fleas in the seat," he responded, "and I'm not sitting there until they're gone."

Tim was a very clean, very hygienic guy, the kind of guy who wore white gloves when he did house work. I tried to reassure him that all the fleas had probably left with Dink, but he would not have any part of that seat.

Bob Migar took the tiller and we returned to inspections. When we returned to quarters, Dink had rid himself of the fleas and was waiting for us, all squeaky clean. Tim wanted to know what chair Dink had sat in, if any, before he showered. We just shook our heads.

Later I saw Tim with a large spray can of flint. He was standing on the side of the ladder staring at the tiller seat, ready to pump and spray the life out of any flea still there.

Houseguests

For some reason lost in time, the quarters of Engine 2 and Ladder 3 is sometimes called "Fort Lafayette." This area of Central Square is frequented by many people who are down on their luck. These unfortunate souls hang around because of the proximity to the shelter and the Salvation Army building. Both these establishments provide food and a place to sleep. When both companies responded to an alarm during the night, the apparatus doors close automatically. We also made it a practice to keep all doors locked; anyone wanting to enter the building could ring the buzzer.

Even though we were very careful, somehow they still got in. It was not unusual to return from a fire and find someone sleeping in your bed. One summer night we returned to quarters and I found a man sitting at my desk on the second floor. When I asked him what he was doing, he replied that he was "Just lookin' around." I politely helped him out the door.

Another time a police cruiser brought back a rubber turnout coat they caught a guy wearing in Central Square. He told them that he'd thought about taking some boots, but it wasn't raining at the time. When they asked him why he didn't steal a helmet, he replied, "Waddaya think I'm crazy! I don't want to look like no fireman."

You never knew where they would be. One morning I opened the door of the ladder truck to place my gear on the seat and a visitor fell out into my arms. He told me that "Those fire engine seats are real comfortable." Another morning Dan Maloney of

Ladder 3 started his pick-up and began his trip home after completing a night tour. He was out on the highway when he heard a tapping on the rear window. He turned around and saw a man in the back of his truck. Dan learned that the man was homeless and had crawled into the truck and fallen to sleep. They guy wanted to know if Dan would take him home too. Dan told me that he considered the guy's request but decided his wife Ann might have trouble understanding.

Not everyone who hung around the area of the firehouse was homeless, of course.

There was a public telephone in front of quarters, and at the time we didn't have a private line in the station. The guys started complaining that every time they went to use the pay phone, a different girl would be in the phone booth. We started watching and sure enough a girl would stand near the phone and answer it when it rang. She would then proceed to cross Massachusetts Avenue to the liquor store, buy a bottle, and then wait for the John to pick her up. A few minute later, a different girl would be stationed by the phone booth. Occasionally one of them would come into quarters and say, "Harry's wife is on the phone and wants to talk to him."

Eventually the chain of command notified the police department who informed the vice squad who shut down the operation. Later they told us there was a guy in a joint further up Mass. Ave. who was making all the arrangements. As the police arrested him he started yelling that he knew who tipped off the cops and there'd be "no more freebies."

One day about three months later, I was standing in front of the station when a very young and pretty girl came up to me. I would say that she was about sixteen or seventeen, but the language that came out of her mouth and was directed toward me would have made a salty sailor blush. "You fucken firemen," she began, "are a bunch of no good chiselling bastards! How the fuck," she continued, "am I supposed to eat?" I told her that the five and dime store down the block was hiring. For a split second she thought of hitting me with her pocketbook. Shaking my finger at her I said, "Don't do it, girly, unless you like the House of Correction." She was so angry that she just stood there and shook.

Then she turned and walked away from me, down the street, in high heels over which she did not yet have full control. That was the last I ever saw of her, and as she tried to strut away in her heels I hoped that she would somehow change her life, that it would not be wasted, that it would not be consumed by the street.

Captain Crawford's Cake

The word was out—Captain Crawford was going to be promoted to deputy chief. He was a good firefighter and officer, and he will be an excellent chief. There would be a party. Plans would be made. The party would be at Lafayette Square, quarters for Ladder 3 and Engine 2. He was commanding officer of Ladder 3 and had been detailed to the car as acting deputy while awaiting his promotion.

Friday night was selected as the big night, and preparations were complete. I was the lieutenant of Engine 2 and would be on duty that night. Friends were invited; other companies in the division would be dropping by to offer their congratulations. The other division chief had agreed to take all boxes and we would be able to celebrate.

At seven in the evening, the new chief arrived with his aide, Dennis. The loafing room behind the apparatus was completely decorated with red and blue crepe paper. A linen tablecloth, donated by a thoughtful wife, covered the table. And on the table was the cake. It was a magnificent cake. White, red and blue frosting. A ladder truck of red frosting was centered on a frosting street. There were signs and trees and clouds overhead. One of the lads knew a baker in East Cambridge who'd made this wonderful cake. It was really something to see. There would be cake for everyone.

The ice cream was softened and ready; the scoops were prepared. Knives and forks were placed beside red napkins. What a party we'd have to celebrate this good man's promotion...Yes!

No.

As the soon-to-be Chief Crawford gazed at the cake, his aide, Dennis—who was also his brother—said, "Boy, that is some cake. I don't think I've ever seen so much detail in a cake. Even in a wedding cake. It's a shame Rose and the kids won't get to see it."

"You know, you're right, Dennis!" he responded, and as we all stood there with our mouths open, hanging, he told Dennis to put the cake into the trunk of the car, that he'll bring it home tomorrow and let the family see it.

There was dead silence in the room—except for the heavy breathing of those who wanted a piece of that cake, a cake they would never see again. When Crawford's gang finished with it, there would be only crumbs, only crumbs. At first we thought he was kidding, but he wasn't. The cake went home and so did the other invited guests. We did eat the ice cream, of course, but it wasn't the same, not the same at all. We wanted ice cream and *cake*.

Dennis left Captain Crawford off at his house the next morning. They took the cake out of the trunk and placed it in the middle of the kitchen table. Rose had already packed his suitcase, and off the Crawford family went—for a two week vacation in Maine. Unfortunately, the now vacationing captain forgot to take the cake.

People say that for quite awhile the Crawfords had the fattest mice in Cambridge.

Round and Round She Goes

One Sunday morning I left the Central Square station early because we had a big day at home coming up. Lieutenant Marks came in early to relieve me. The square was quiet, probably because of the early hour and the late hours people tend to keep on Saturday night. I entered the subway fully expecting an uneventful ride to Harvard Square. No teller was working on the side I used to enter; in order to get to the train platform, I would have to pass through an enclosed, upright turnstile, the kind that went from dirty floor to dirty ceiling and looked like a vertical carpet sweeper brush. No problem. You pay your fare, make a half turn through the cage, and you are on the inside of the platform waiting for your train! Easy as pie...a cakewalk...but not for me. I inserted my fare, pushed against the turnstile and found myself in prison.

Apparently the chain that prevents passengers from entering the wrong side of the turnstile was missing, and I had inadvertently entered the wrong side, and it had only turned a quarter of the way. I could not go forward or backward. I was trapped! As I said, it was a quiet Sunday morning, so few people were in the station at that hour of the morning who might be interested in my plight. So there I stood in full Cambridge Fire Department uniform, stuck in a turnstile.

I noticed someone I reasoned was a drunk sleeping on a platform bench. I called to him and called to him until he finally awakened. He staggered over to my prison cell and, scratching his head, said, "Well, I guess that now I have seen everything!

Now you've gotta pay to get a fireman if you need one!" That social observation made, he walked off, shaking his head as he made his way unassuredly down the platform.

After what seemed an eternity, an elderly lady came along. I gave her a smile of Sunday morning Christian fellowship and asked if she could help me out of this predicament. She stood with her back to me as I tried to explain how this situation had come about. I could not be sure that she was actually listening to me. Finally, she agreed to inform the train conductor of my problem. She turned her back to me and returned to her silent stance.

When the train did arrive, she did inform the conductor of my predicament. Everyone on the train watched the process of my rescue with much interest as the conductor proceeded to go through a ring of at least two hundred keys. He then said, "We may have to call the fire department to get you out."

"Oh no you don't!" I bellowed. "No way! Just keep going through those keys."

Finally he found the right key and I was a free man. Before taking a seat on the train, I humbly thanked the lady who had initiated my rescue. She turned to me with glaring eyes and hissed, *"Masher!* Get away from me before I call the conductor!" I must also tell you that it was a very long ride into Harvard Square, even though Harvard was the next subway stop; few of the train's passengers appreciated the delay I had caused them.

At least when I got home Peggy was a bit more sympathetic...but she still laughed!

The Riots—1968

In terms of domestic tranquility, the United States had seen better years than 1968. It was a year of national unrest, particularly in our cities. The Vietnam War was raging, and protests against the United States' government's policies were escalating, especially among college and university student populations. Since the City of Cambridge plays host to both Harvard University and the Massachusetts Institute of Technology, the city has a large student population. The tension between these young angry and dissatisfied people and their perceived authority figures seemed almost palpable. I was a fire lieutenant, an employee and representative of the government, and although it didn't make any sense to me, I guess they were against me and my troops, too.

I was stationed at Engine 6, located west of Central Square, and although this was a residential, primarily tenement area, we were only about three miles from Harvard University. A few of their buildings were within our inspection duty. We had seen Viet Cong flags on bulletin boards and attached to walls during our inspections tours. The incidence of false alarms on the Harvard campus was steadily increasing and sometimes Viet Cong flags were waved at us as we returned to quarters. We knew, therefore, that serious trouble was brewing, that the storm clouds were gathering fast. We began responding to bomb threats on a daily basis. And then some Harvard students took over one of the university buildings used for R.O.T.C. The police arrested many students. Retaliation was inevitable. We had entered an urban war zone.

A good friend of mine, Dan Murphy, was a photographer for a big Boston newspaper, and he told me that he would let me know if trouble was imminent. We had already been issued riot shields that attached to our helmets, wrap-around plastic visors that were designed to protect the eyes. When I reported for duty Saturday morning, the lieutenant whom I was relieving told me trouble was on the way. Shortly after that I got a call from the division deputy chief who informed me that we were to put on the helmet shields and to stand by for announced running card assignment changes. Boxes would only be struck for actual building fires; all other incidents would be treated on a reduced assignment basis.

At about ten a.m. Dan called me on the outside phone and told me that thousands of demonstrators were gathering on the Boston Common, and as far as he could determine, Cambridge was to be their destination and target. When I went back inside to tell the boys the news, Johnny Park handed me the phone. It was the division chief: "Lieutenant," he said, "we now have official information that a very large crowd of protestors will cross over the Harvard Bridge into Cambridge on Massachusetts Avenue. The police aren't sure of the plan, but they suspect the target is either city hall or Harvard Square."

I hung up the phone and said, "Looks like it's heading towards the fan, John!"

We were running a two piece company, hose tender and pumper. John and I were on the pump, and Joe Scanlon, Charlie Butler and Bill Rodley on the wagon. We waited and watched the police cars passing the firehouse at a steady clip. A reduced assignment signal sounded on the primary house gong. John made the proper entry into the company journal and we waited for further developments. We didn't have to wait very long. A police cruiser stopped on the apron and a cop came in to use the men's room. He informed us that he and his partner would he staging from the firehouse. He also informed us that Engine 2 and Ladder 3, located on Mass. Ave. near the bridge, were blocked in by people and will never be able to get out the door. This meant that we would be covering the entire south side of the City of Cambridge. According to the officer, the crowd extended from Cambridge City Hall to the bridge—a five block long procession of angry young people sidewalk to sidewalk on a six lane main drag.

I told the boys to put their lunch bags aboard the rigs since we had no way of knowing where we'd end up. I think I was being optimistic and perhaps trying to make our situation seem less bizarre than it actually was and would be. We listened to the police radio and heard that it was now fairly certain that Harvard Square was the demonstrators' target. About ten minutes later the police cruiser took off on an assignment. Just after they left the firehouse, we received the audible that Fire Alarm was striking Box 5134 for a building fire in Brattle Square, which is a major intersection adjacent to the Harvard Square area.

We headed up Memorial Drive toward Harvard Square. When we got to Boylston Street, about two hundred Metropolitan District Commission police officers in full riot gear were staged at the corner of Memorial Drive and Boylston Street. They broke ranks and allowed us to enter Boylston. Now I could see the smoke and flame. It was the Northeast Federal Savings Bank building, and it was fully involved. Flames were coming from the front windows; it had been firebombed. Division Chief Haley was standing in front of the building yelling, "*No firefighting—no firefighting!* Return to quarters. Suddenly the air was full of flying objects, missiles. I realized that we were being bricked. The wagon was enclosed, but the pump was open cab.

I couldn't believe it, but all I could see was people throwing sidewalk bricks at us. John was able to turn the rig around. Fortunately, the hose wagon has a very short wheel base and could turn around quickly. We were being hit bad. A brick crashed through the windshield and struck John squarely in the face shield, then bounced off and hit me on the left shoulder. John slumped in the driver's seat, blood pouring from his face. The pump jumped the curb and we hit a brick wall.

Then we were surrounded. The rioters were pulling at us. I had no doubt that these well educated young boys and girls meant to kill us. The windshield was gone; glass was everywhere. My eyes had glass in them and I tried not to blink.

All I could see was crazed people. John raised his head and re-started the engine. "**Go, go, go!**" I yelled to John. We were back on the street and moving. Bricks fell down on us like a hurricane's rain. I couldn't look back to see how the hose wagon made out—all I could do was hope.

When we broke through the police lines on Memorial Drive, I knew that we'd made it. Fortunately, the wagon was right behind us. The windshield was badly cracked but not broken; Joe and Charlie were OK. Rodley had been riding the rear step; when the bricks began to fly, he'd squirmed between the hose and the deck boards. This saved him from serious injury, possibly even death.

John had been a tank commander during World War II; he'd been awarded the Silver Star for bravery. He saved his crew when they were hit by German fire. I do believe that he saved our lives by getting us to hell out of the square before the rioters killed us.

All hell was breaking loose in the city. Calls for fire were coming in fast and furious, and companies were being dispatched in all directions. Fire Alarm called us for another assignment, but I told them that we were out of service due to injuries. I didn't like the way John looked; he was as pale as a ghost. I drove the pump back to quarters. In front of the firehouse was a police car on the end of a tow hook—on fire. I told the tow truck driver to take the car down the street and drop it in the Charles River.

We backed the apparatus into quarters. We were really hurting; blood was running down John's face and he was semi-conscious. I called Fire Alarm on the phone and requested that the Rescue unit be dispatched to our quarters. The brick that hit John had bounced off his face shield and hit my left shoulder which now hurt like hell. We learned later that girls were digging the bricks out of the sidewalk, breaking them in half with brick hammers, and carrying them in knapsacks. They were the ammunition carriers for the male maggots who were throwing the bricks.

Charlie and Joe were in the cab of the wagon and weren't hurt. All the windows were cracked, but the glass was still in place.

The Rescue took John to the hospital. I put my head under the faucet in the kitchen sink and was able to wash out most of the glass in my eyes. We received the "full riot" signal on the primary gongs. This meant that all runs would be given by radio or telephone and police protection would be provided. We were dispatched by phone to meet the police at Massachusetts Avenue and Bay Street. Bill drove the pump. As we responded, the sidewalks on both sides of Mass. Ave. were packed with people. When we reached the location, Sgt. Orr of the Cambridge Police Department informed me that a bomb was in the car. I informed Sgt. Orr that I knew little about bombs, and the little I did know was to stay the hell away from them. The sergeant used his radio to inform his dispatcher to notify the State Police Bomb Squad. We cleared the incident and were immediately sent to a staging location near Harvard Square. As we headed towards the staging location, we encountered two police cruisers tipped over on Putnam Avenue; the vehicles had not been set on fire. We checked the cars and found no police officers inside—a happy discovery.

Even before we arrived at the staging area, we received another call: "Engine 6. Respond to check for a fire in St. Paul's Church on Bow Street." Bow Street served as the unofficial southern border of the Harvard Square area; it was not a location we wanted to visit on this day since we knew that there were major riot conditions in the square. Fire Alarm also informed us that Ladder 1 had been surrounded on Dunster Street and the crew had to run for their lives. All axes, hooks, wrenches, any piece of equipment that could be used to cause damage were stolen.

St. Paul's Church was three blocks away from where Ladder 1 was stranded. We stopped near the intersection of Mass. and Putnam Avenues; I had no intention of bringing the apparatus closer to Harvard Square. I told my crew to stand by while I walked down to check and see if the master box had been tripped. Joe said that he wouldn't let me go alone. As we made our way down Mt. Auburn Street, a member of Ladder 1's crew was running towards us like the devil was chasing him. He told us that the crew was scattered and he was running to save his life. I later learned that he had escaped by taking an elevator in a building of Holyoke Center—an interconnected hi-rise complex in the middle of the square that serves as Harvard's administrative core—and crossing over to another building, then exiting onto a different street.

The master box at St. Paul's was set, which indicated that the box was pulled from outside and the church was not on fire. I'd just finished winding the box when a bullet hit the wall over my head. There was a shower of brick dust. It was time to show them my dust! Joe and I ran like hell back up Mt. Auburn Street toward where the apparatus was parked.

Both the pump and the wagon were surrounded by rioters. My men were nowhere in sight. Across the street riot police were fighting with demonstrators. When they saw me, Bill and Charlie crawled out from under the pump. The crowd started to rock the engine to turn it over. The air was full of flying missiles. It was complete chaos. They were scaling pieces of pipe along the street at the police lines. The pipe would come up under the police riot shield and break the officers' shins.

This was the most fearful night that I ever spent on the Cambridge Fire Department.

I stood up in the pump seat and held up my hand and gave the V for victory sign. Some of the rioters started yelling, "We got the fire department on our side." I suppose it looked as if we were swinging over to their side; I didn't particularly give a rat's ass what they thought as long as we could get out of there alive. The crowd parted and we were able to proceed up Putnam Ave. We passed a small group of police officers who were greatly outnumbered; when the rioters saw the pump jump the curb toward them, they scattered and the officers were able to escape.

The next call we received was for a building fire on Massachusetts Avenue. A Molotov cocktail had been thrown against a store front. The police were right there and called us quickly. Another engine company extinguished the fire and checked for possible extension and we were dismissed.

We'd been running through chaos for about three hours. This time we backed into our quarters. Things seemed to be slowing down. A hot cup of coffee sure tasted good. I tried to call the hospital to see how John was making out, but I couldn't get through. Bill's ankle was quite swollen, but he wanted to stay on duty. We learned later that he'd been driving the pump with a fractured ankle.

During the early hours of the morning two men came into quarters and identified themselves as FBI agents. They had cameras they said they'd used to take photos of the rioters. As we described the events of our day to them and we came to the part about John restarting the pump on Boylston Street, the agent taking notes stopped, looked me straight in the face and said, "I hope you squashed a couple of maggots!" Tough times.

The next day they found six police cars in the Charles River; I guess that at the time it was a good way to put out the fires. All of the glass on the pump control panel was smashed; we even found bricks inside the soft suction hose. The brick that hit John in the face and then hit my shoulder was on the window sill of Engine 6 for some time. I went looking for it one day to show someone, but it had disappeared. Later I heard that one of the guys needed a brick to finish off a barbecue pit in his back yard—a fitting place since it had nearly finished us off.

Some years later Bill was promoted to lieutenant and then to captain. The day that I received my mark on the captain's test, he was the first one over the stairs to congratulate me. We've remained close friends. John died in the line of duty at a fire on Tufts Street in 1971. I was a captain on another engine company, but I was working at the same fire. Charlie had a heart attack in quarters in 1983 and retired. Joe is the only member of my 1968 crew who is still working. He's assigned to a busy engine company.

They were all good men and I think that only a good team effort allowed us to survive that horrible day and night. We could never fully understand why the student rioters tried so hard to hurt us. We were just doing our job. When I walk through Harvard Square today and think back on how it was that night, I get the feeling that the seeds of hate may always be there...but they must not be allowed to grow.

Check the Dumpster

Firefighting in high-rise buildings involves much different strategy than fires in ordinary frame structures. New construction materials and technological advances have helped make the quick control of high-rise fires much easier. For example, in many municipalities buildings over a certain height are required to have sprinkler and standpipe systems.

The use of elevators is vital. Equipment and hose can quickly be brought to the assigned staging area, usually located a few floor beneath the fire. From this point search and rescue operations are conducted. Certain radio frequencies are assigned to the fire command center, and communications between firefighting units are established.

It was a cold, rainy night in October. As I sat at the desk in the office of Ladder 3, I could not help thinking and hoping that there would be no fires tonight. As I looked out the window at the wind swept square, I could see huddled figures leanging against the wind, probably on their way home.

My favortie music station was on the radio and I was giving serious consideration to stretching out for a bit. Sometimes if you can catch a few winks early it will help if you catch a job later. The tone alarm sounded and the lights came on, snapping me back to reality. "Attention Ladder 3 and Engine 2. Respond to a building fire—123 Erie Street. Box 3754 is being struck."

I knew that 123 Erie Street was a high-rise building devoted primarily to housing for the elderly and that it would pose its own unique problems. Assisted evacuation might be necessary because of the age of the occupants. It was early evening and many people were sitting down to supper.

When we arrived at the scene, the lobby was already becoming crowded with occupants since no one wanted to go out in the rain. The alarm panel indicated an activation on the seventeenth floor. One of the custodians approached me and said, "Captain, people are calling my office to report that there was smoke on the upper floors." Many times smoke conditions during meal hours turn out to be nothing more than burnt food. However, we assume nothing; we always conduct operations as if we were going to encounter a fire.

Using the special key, we placed an elevator on fire command. This means we can control the elevator. Engine 2 and Ladder 3 loaded equipment on and we proceeded up to the fifteenth floor. The high-rise standard operating procedure stipulates that we establish an advance base of operation two floors below the fire, if this is possible. From this point various units are assigned operational tasks such as search and rescue and firefighting.

There was a light haze of smoke on the sixteenth floor. Engine 2 started to connect to the standpipe in the stairway. We banged on some doors and helped a few people to the emergency exit stairs. The noise level of the building's fire alarm system was enough to blow your mind. I couldn't imagine anyone could sleep through it. I guess they it kept excessively loud to make certain that everyone will hear it. Smoke was starting to bank down and we completed a primary search of that floor. Now we could hardly see the hall ceiling lights. Thank God for self-contained breathing apparatus which allow us to finish our search. Fire command called me for a report on conditions. The smoke was now on the floor level and visability was zero. Using the hallway wall as a guide, we found the fire tower stairway. Engine 2 advanced a two and a half inch line up the stairs to the fire floor. As they advanced the line down the hall toward the fire, we started searching rooms for anyone who might be trapped. It was getting very hot and my ears were starting to cook. Adance command advised me that fire was blowing out three windows on the north corner of the fire floor. This was good news; it meant that the fire had vented itself. We were now operating with a second alarm assignment. Extra manpower would be needed for fire operations and for relief.

A little way down the hall we could hear someone yelling, "Help! Help!" we found the door; it was closed. An elderly lady is inside the apartment and she is in a state of panic. The door was metal clad and smoke tight. To open the door at this point would be a mistake. Smoke conditions in the hall are very bad. Through the closed door we tell the woman that she is safe and we are here. I calmed her down and told her to open the apartment windows for additional air. Her voice was lower now and seemed to display less panic. I asked her what she had for supper.

Things were slowly improving down the hallway. They were getting water on the fire. I could see the hall ceiling lights. The rest of my crew had completed the search of the floor with negative results.

My lady friend had calmed down considerably and now informed me that she is eighty-three and her husband is eighty-eight and in a wheel chair. She also thinks firemen are great; she wanted to be one when she was a little girl in Texas. When it was safe to move them, we opened the door she gave me a big hug. She and her husband were taken down to the fifteenth floor and then by elevator to the ground floor.

Then I noticed that someone had finally shut off that damned alarm horn. "Praise the Lord!" I yelled. "Now maybe we can hear ourselves think." Shortly after this, the engine crews report the fire is knocked down and overhauling began.

Relief crews are now on the fire floor and take the hoses. Our air is pretty well used up and we go to advance command on the fifteenth floor. We take a blow and change cylinders, then return to the fire floor. The fire apartment is a mess. Walls are black and burnt furniture is all over the place. The chief informed me that a man lived alone in this apartment. Every nook and corner of the apartment is searched—no man is found. The Fire Investigation Unit determined that the fire started in the vicinity of the stove.

The chief dismissed us at 7:30 and we returned to quarters. I had a feeling that it was going to be one of those nights so I had a quick cup of coffee and then headed up to the office to do some paperwork. However, except for a couple of false alarms, the remainder of the tour was quiet. And then at about 1 a.m. the phone rang.

It was Chief Muligan; he asked me if I checked the dumpster in the rear of the building for a body. He explained that the dumpster was located right under the windows of the fire apartment and since no one could locate the apartment's occupant, there was a real possibility that he could have jumped and landed in the dumpster. We still alarm ourselves out to check the dumpster.

As we drove back to the 123 Erie Street I could not help thinking that if a body is in the dumpster, then someone will have to do some tall explaining. With thumping hearts we climbed up the dumpster and looked inside. Lots of rubbish—no jumper. I reported our findings to the chief, had another cup of coffee and went to bed.

The next day tour Chief Muligan called to inform me that our missing friend was on a toot in Boston and did return safe and sound. The chief also informed me that the occupant wanted a full investigation and the names of the people who messed up his pad.

A Church Full of Angels

I was sitting at the desk of Ladder 3 on Sunday morning making out the morning report. We were having a very heavy rain and lightning storm—the kind of ferocious tempest we get during the summer months. Looking out the second floor window I saw a bolt of lightning strike the steeple of the church on Main Street about a block away. I called Fire Alarm and told them to strike a box to send more engines to the scene. When we arrived at the church we found smoke and fire showing from the steeple. The church was a fairly large building of wood construction.

The church was also filled with Sunday worshippers. The front door was jammed tight and would not open, and we could hear yelling and pounding on the door. Using forcible entry tools, we were able to open the door and very frightened people tumbled out. We conducted a search and made sure that everyone was out of the building.

The fire involved only a small section of the steeple and we extinguished it quickly. One of the ushers told me that he had been standing at the rear of the church with his hands on a radiator as Reverend Mr. Jones, the visiting preacher from Boston, was calling on the Lord to come down and be with us. The usher said he could feel the presence of the Lord as the electricity passed from the radiator through his body. He told me that Lord sure came down, but he hoped there was not too much damage to the steeple.

Man's Best Friend!

It was a cold night in February and we were told to respond to the Charles River to assist the Rescue Company. Fire Alarm had received a call that a dog was in the river. When we arrived, the police were at the scene and told us that a dog was frozen in the ice near the river's bank. The dog looked like he was finished. He was laying on his side and was almost frozen stiff. We used the axe to free him, Rescue wrapped him in a blanket and placed him in the cab of the piece. When we arrived back at the firehouse, we placed him gently on a blanket near the radiator in the patrol room. The police said that they would notify the proper people to pick up the dog.

I'd been doing paperwork upstairs for about a half hour when I heard a hell of a commotion on the first floor. As I reached the landing I saw one of my men running wild-eyed up the stairs and yelling, "Mad dog, mad dog!!!" Right on his heels was the dog.

He chased me, the crews of Rescue, Ladder 1 and Engine 1, the chief's aide and the chief around headquarters—up the stairs, down the stairs for at least ten minutes, all the time barking like a hound from hell. Finally the dog ran out steam and we were able to steer him into an unused closet. "How's that for gratitude," I said. "We save his frozen little hide from the river and he wants to have us for supper!"

The guys from the Animal Rescue League finally showed up and took the dog away. We never did find out if the dog was trying to thank us or bite us.

Joe

I worked with Joe Rodgers at Lafayette Square. He was the lieutenant on the truck and I was captain of the engine company. We became very close and often had long discussions on many subjects. I like to think that Joe let me see a side of his character that only a few people ever saw.

Not far from our station was a shelter for homeless people. Each eveing at about six the patrons started to gather near the shelter; first only a few, then more would come. Some pushed shopping carts filled with all they owned. Others had only the clothes they had on their backs. There were men and women of all ages and races, all having one thing in common—nowhere to stay the night. When I had the first watch they would be there, looking in the apparatus door window in front of the station. There were many sorry sights. Sometimes a whole family, with small kids, would be waiting patiently for the shelter to open. We heated many baby bottles, and we frequently provided the milk.

Joe never had much to say to me about the unfortunate people. One cold and snowy night I was having a cup of coffee in the kitchen at the rear of the apparatus floor and I noticed a group waiting outside, then I noticed Joe taking them all in. As I walked toward the front of the building I saw what he was doing. He was giving each one money and holding his finger to his lips, signalling them to be silent. He didn't see me and I never let him know that I knew his little secret.

I can remember another time when Joe played the role of

Good Samaritan. One night he and I were looking out the window watching "Saint Joseph" make his selections as to who would get a spot in the shelter. We called this shelter employee "Saint Joseph" because of the way he would wave his hand to indicate the people he had chosen for the night. His decision was usually predicated on the fact the he would not allow troublemakers into the shelter, and some of those standing before him had, on other occasions, given him trouble.

Joe spotted a young girl, perhaps about eighteen years old, standing to the side of the station. Saint Joseph could not see her because she was out of his line of vision behind an automobile. After he made his selections, he started to move his little flock toward the shelter. They were a sorry collection with their shopping carts and grocery bags, some large, some small, containing all of their worldly possessions.

The girl was left behind crying. Just then the engine was dispatched to investigate a fuel spill on Cherry Street. We were gone about ten minutes. When we returned there was no on in front of the station.

About a week later, a well-dressed, middle-aged man entered quarters and wanted to thank the fire officer who had been so kind to his daughter. The girl had run off with a serviceman in New York, and he had abandoned her in Boston. While we were gone on the still alarm Joe had talked to her and she'd told him what had happened. He contacted the shelter and made arrangements for her to spend the night there. The shelter had contacted the girl's parents. Now the girl's father wanted to repay the five dollars Joe had given to her.

I was on vacation when Joe went down. It was a two bagger in a three story frame on Prospect Street. The day was hot and Joe was a worker; he and his company had opened the roof and thrown ladders. As he was coming down the rear stairs from the third floor on the way out to get a fresh air cylinder, he had a massive heart attack.

I went to see him the next day in the intensive care unit of the hospital. He smiled at me and said, "Well, Cap, I guess this is the end of my career." He was right—it was the end. He pensioned out on disability. About six weeks after he was retired he showed up at my house with a bag of uniform shirts for me. We sat down and my wife made us some coffee. He wanted to know the latest happenings on the job. After I filled him in on the real and the hearsay, I asked him what he was doing with himself. "You're not going to believe this, Cap," he replied, "but I'm going to train to become a deacon in my church." I believed it with all my heart.

Joe called me about four months later and asked me to speak for him at his ordination. It was a small church. The flickering candles cast dancing shadows on the ceiling. The choir was in place and gently swaying back and forth as they sang the gospel music. The ministers were on the altar and all was ready...and there was Joe.

I don't think I could actually describe the look of happiness on his face. His eyes were closed and he was in deep prayer. Now it was my turn to speak. I made my way to the altar and stood before the congregation. The words came so easily as I told them of the Joe who was my fellow firefighter and my friend. He sat there with his head bowed and rocked ever so slightly back and forth. I knew things about Joe, the real Joe.

About three months later I received a call from Joe's wife Gladys—Joe had died. The wake was held in his church. The choir was there, gently clapping their hands as they sang a farewell. The song they sang was Frank Sinatra's "My Way"; they had changed the lyrics to "Joe did it his way." Two dozen fully uniformed firefighters sat in the front pews. Joe was laid out in the white robes of a deacon. The flickering candles reflected on his peaceful face, which seemed to me to have a slight smile.

This time I did not speak; there was little to say.

This Diamond Ring

One evening a guy walked into Engine7's quarters and asked Joe Daily if he want to buy a diamond ring. This station is located near the Longfellow Bridge that connects Cambridge to Boston, so it was not unusual for us to have folks who looked like they belonged in Downtown Boston drop in on us occasionally. It was a woman's ring, one that would probably be given for an engagement. The fellow was young, his clothes were of good quality, and he seemed to possess a certain refined bearing. He also did not look very happy. He seemed to have made a major decision.

Joe yelled out to the kitchen if anyone was interested in the purchase. The other two men on duty came out and examined the ring. "Piece of glass!" was one opinion. I was sitting at the table near the watch desk and Joe called over to me, "Hey, Captain, you want to buy a ring?" I just shook my head.

Joe contemplated the ring and asked, "How much you want?" The fellow replied that he wanted to get home and selling the ring was the only way. He was asking fifty dollars. I asked him where he lived. "Walpole, Mass.," he replied. It was about nine o'clock at night; we offered to give him the bus fare home. His response was that he was not interested in charity, he only wanted to sell the ring. Of course, it was possible he could have stolen the ring or that it was just a piece of glass, but he didn't look like a thief or a con artist. He just looked like a young, sad guy who had to make a major transition in his life...and then go home.

Joe finally said that he would loan the guy twenty-five dollars and hold the ring for security. The fellow accepted the deal, gave Joe the ring, took the money and left the quarters of Engine 7 walking back towards the Longfellow Bridge, back towards Boston.

Time passed and we forgot about the incident. Then one day Joe came to work and told us that he gone to a jeweler and had the ring appraised. The jeweler informed Joe that the ring was genuine, that it was worth $3,000. Needless to say we were amazed. "Piece of glass" indeed!

Joe had reported the incident to the police, but there'd been no report of a lost or stolen ring during that period of time. We never saw the young man again. I often wondered why he never came back for his ring—especially after we learned its actual worth. Joe kept the ring...he never sold it.

Just a Boy

During the hot summer months of June, July and August, we would be very busy responding to false alarms. The general area of East Cambridge south of the railroad tracks would really keep us hopping. In some cases we would be responding from one box to another. The real danger in this is the possibility that a call for an actual fire could be received and the apparatus would be tied up at a false alarm. Fire Alarm would then have to dispatch engines from another district, resulting in a serious delay in response time.

This happened many times during my career, and it happened once with tragic results. We were just clearing a series of false alarms when Fire Alarm called us by radio and ordered us to respond to a building fire on Columbia Street. A full first alarm assignment was dispatched—three engines, two ladder companies, the Rescue, and a deputy chief. We were only two blocks away, and as we approached the location I could tell that something strange was going on. People were running in all directions and screaming, screaming uncontrollably from fear or horror. Then up near the corner of Columbia and Cambridge Streets I could see a running ball of flame. It was a person on fire.

A woman screamed at me, pleaded with me to help. "Oh, God, help him! Help him!" She was not, however, pointing at the running ball of fire, but to the doorway of a four story row house. Other apparatus were arriving. The officer of the truck yelled to me that he'd chase the burning victim in the street. It was mass confusion. My men were running a line to back me up. A long hallway led to the rear of the apartment and as I walked through the hallway I kept wondering, *What the hell is going on?* There was a haze of black soot in the hall and a black smudge on the wallpaper. To the left was a living room, people sitting on a couch, looking at me. A man said, "Down the hallway...he's down the hallway in the kitchen."

A boy about fifteen years old lay on his back on the floor in front of the kitchen sink. His skin was sizzling. Long black hair was burnt and matted to his face. Each time he tried to move his arms I could hear the skin crack. My crew were beside me. They began wetting him down. He was horribly burnt over most of his body. I took off my helmet and knelt down beside him. Pure panic filled his eyes. He was saying, "I told him not to light the match...not to light...Oh Jesus! Am I burnt bad?"

They were cleaning motor bike parts while sitting on the stoop in front of the building. One stood up to light a cigarette, his hands were soaked in gasoline, there was a ball of fire. One ran up the street; I was kneeling beside the other. The pan full of gas had tipped over onto his lap.

His eyes fixed on mine. "Am I bad, mister?" he asked. "Am I bad?" Each time he opened his mouth, I could see that the inside was also burnt. "My name is Jerry Long," he replied to my question. The Rescue guys were now with us. They poured sterile water on the boy and wrapped him in wet dressing. He was so scared. When I whispered in his ear that he was not burnt bad at all and that he would make it, his eyes lit up and he tried to smile at me. His voice was distorted by his shivering body. "I can't breathe. I can't breathe, mister!" I held his hand as they placed him on the litter.

The other lad who was burnt was attended to by other crews and transported to the hospital; I never saw him but they told me he was also badly burnt. It was a flash fire and did not involve the building. The people on the couch were in shock. They had told the boys not to use gasoline so close to the building. Jerry's intention was to get to the kitchen and put out the fire, but he never made it. Both boys died on the way to the Mass. General Hospital. Their lungs were burnt. They didn't have a chance.

We were dismissed and returned to quarters. We all just sat

there in the loafing room and drank coffee in silence. I had trouble sleeping for awhile. I could see Jerry's face and I could hear his voice asking me, "Am I bad, mister? Am I bad?"

Out of the Closet

As I sat at my desk in my office on the third floor of the East Cambridge Station, I heard a strange noise. This is a large building that houses Engine Company/Foam 3 and Ladder Company 2. The training division also has classrooms and offices on the third floor. The noise sounded like tapping and sometimes like pounding. When I went into the training division to ask them what they were fixing, Deputy Chief Allis assured me that they weren't doing anything but watching some new training films.

I returned to my office and resumed my paperwork; I heard the sounds again. The house work is done floor by floor, and all hands were working on the apparatus floor so I knew it wasn't a noise made from cleaning. But there it was again! It seemed to be coming from somewhere down the hall. I followed the sound and saw little scraps of paper on the floor. I picked one up and read, "HELP, MY NAME IS CLAUDE REDMUND, I AM LOCKED IN THE CLOSET, I CAN'T GET OUT. PLEASE HELP!" I picked up another piece of paper: "Help! Help! Still in the closet." The trail of notes led to a utility closet used to wash out mops and buckets. On the floor was a small pile of papers that apparently came from under the door.

Getting down on my hands and knees, I peeked under the door and saw Claude blowing paper out. I could see his white teeth grinning at me. I opened the door and there he was—stripped down to his shorts. He hugged me and said, "Oh

Captain, my Captain, you're my savior." He had removed all the paneling in his efforts to escape. He was covered with sweat, but aside from a few scratches he was fine.

The door knob on the door to the utility closet was defective; I had requested many times that it be replaced. As a stopgap, the latch had been taped to prevent the door from locking, but apparently the tape had broken which allowed the door to close behind Claude while he was washing out a mop in the basin. Everyone else had finished their work on the third floor and gone down to the apparatus floor.

Claude was very happy that I was doing my paperwork while he was doing his.

A Lesson

Part of recruit training was done at Engine 3, East Cambridge Station. There was a class in progress at this time. All the recruits were in the kitchen during the coffee break. I sat down for a cup of coffee with them and asked how the training was coming along. They replied that the subject at hand was the proper method of overhauling.

One of the basic rules of overhauling is that possible evidence of arson must be protected and not tossed out a window. One of the recruits asked me, "Hey, Captain, how did they handle overhauling back when you were a rookie?" My reply took the form of a story.

One cold winter morning I reported for duty only to find a covering Boston company in our station. There was a four alarm fire in progress on Clark Street near Broadway. We changed into our working clothes and the lieutenant told us to dress warm. "There's no telling how long you'll be there, guys," he added. The hose wagon was sent back for us. Harry Ford jumped down from the driver's seat and I saw that he was covered with debris and his face was black from smoke. His eyes were bloodshot and mucus was hanging from his nose.

Harry stood there trying to unlock his rubber coat. "Shit!" he hissed. "I have to take a piss real bad." There was no time to thaw out the snaps. Poor Harry stood there on the apparatus floor and pissed in his night hitch.

The street was covered with ice and there were few spectators at the fire. The fire building was a four story duplex and it had been heavily involved. We followed our line through a maze of hose, plaster, burnt wood and run-off water. Our guys were overhauling on the third floor, which meant they were checking for any hidden fire and throwing debris out the window. We found a few hot spots in the dining room ceiling and the ladder men opened so we could hit it with water.

After working for about two hours, we were told to take a breather and get a coffee. The rear stairs were closest, so down we went. The door led to an alley. Smokey Joe Stover yelled in a loud, clear voice, "Man coming out!" and up the alley he ran. Now it was my turn and in the timid whisper of a rookie I state the fact that I am about to leave the building.

After one step I was hit on the top of the head with a king size mattress that had sailed down from the top floor. The water soaked missile drove my helmet down over my eyes and fractured my nose. It took six strong nurses to pull it off. My neck was almost broken and I had to wear a Thomas collar for three weeks.

My eyes searched the attentive audience before me. I had their undivided attention. "Go on, Cap, what happened next?"

"Well, boys," I continued, "being hit on the head was bad enough, but I had to pay out good money to have all my pants shortened. You see, I went from being five feet-nine in my stock feet to five feet-six."

For a long moment there was just silence, and then one of them started to chuckle, saying, "Come on, Cap, you're kiddin'. You don't expect us to buy that?"

As I got up from the table I responded that I was not kidding and that he could buy whatever he liked, but to this day I was very thankful that it was not a piano.

Those Socks

We had another spark, a fellow named Leon, who slept in quarters on weekends. He was a big man who worked very, very hard. One day one of my men informed me that the spark's feet were driving them out of the bunk room. I guess that Leon would come to the station directly from his job—no shower, no clean clothes, no clean socks. I said I would sniff around and see what this was all about, which I never actually did. About a month later, the same firefighter came to see me again and complained again. This time he said that if I continued to "kick it under the table", he'd have to side step me and go to the division chief. This, of course, put me in a very awkward position. I liked Leon; the thought of hurting him did not appeal to me.

Seizing the bull by the socks, I started a conversation with Leon about his job. We talked for several minutes, then he turned to me and said, "Hey, Captain, you don't need to worry. I'll wash my feet and change my socks before I come to the firehouse." My jaw dropped. How did he know? I just had to ask him. Leon folded his hands in his lap, crossed his thumbs, looked down at the floor and said that the smell was waking him up too.

Not very long after that incident we had a very tough fire in a manufacturing building. The Rescue Company entered the loading dock area through a side door to see if they could open an overhead garage door. The door they entered, however, could not be opened from the inside and locked behind them. The main body of fire was in the rear of the building and spreading toward the front. We were standing by with a two and a half inch line, ready to advance once the garage door was opened. Conditions rapidly deteriorated. The walls were bulging with heavy black smoke. It was impossible for Rescue to reach the front overhead garage doors; they were trapped behind the door that they had entered. "May Day! May Day! Rescue trapped, front of building, Sydney Street side." Things were now very, very bad, and quickly getting worse. Then someone yelled, "It's going to blow." My heart sank—I knew that they were in deep trouble.

Leon heard the May Day. Taking a ten pound sledge hammer from the ladder truck parked in front of the building, he started beating on the locked door. He was totally transfixed, beating the hell out of the door. No one dared go near him. The door was falling apart under the smashing blows. Soon the it gave way and Captain Collins and his crew crawled out. Our line was charged and ready. The backdraft blew the overhead doors across Sydney Street. The flames were now burning the power lines across the street.

It was a close call for the Rescue guys. All their alarm bells were ringing, indicating that they were out of air. They later thanked Leon and told him that he was welcome in their station any time...socks or no socks.

Tight Skirt

At 3:00 a.m. we received a call for a house fire in a multiple occupancy rooming house on Prospect Street. At about nine o'clock that evening there had been a fire in a mattress in one of the rooms. A resident "extinguished" the fire and everyone returned to bed. Unfortunately, this procedure had a couple of problems: first, the fire department was never called; second, you cannot put out a mattress fire using a limited amount of water.

The rekindlings of supposedly extinguished mattress fires have taken many lives and cost millions of dollars in fire damage. The only way to extinguish a mattress fire is to take it to a hydrant, tear it apart and soak the hell out of it. People usually think they have the fire out, but the mattress ticking will smolder and ignite when they are tucked back in their beds.

This is exactly what happened on Prospect Street. They had left the mattress leaning against the wall in the main front entry way. When we arrived at the scene, the entire front of the building was burning. The fire was extending up the front stairs, cutting off all escape for the residents of the rooming house.

People were hanging from every window. I was captain of the first arriving ladder truck and I knew immediately we had a serious fire with a tremendous possibility of loss of life. I ordered a second alarm the minute I arrived. A police officer was yelling at us that people were trapped on the roof of the right side of the building. Another cop told me that a man was getting ready to jump from the window on the second floor of the other side. I could hear breaking glass and screaming. Here I was with a three man ladder company—and this included me! We had lots of ladders but no one to throw them. The engine company that arrived simultaneously with us also had three men, and they were desperately trying to get water on the fire. A properly placed hose line will always save more lives than spectacular rescues.

More apparatus arrived, and a third and fourth alarms were sounded in rapid order. Larry had pulled a thirty-five foot ladder off all by himself and was going after the guy getting ready to jump from the window. Lucky and I were throwing a thirty-five footer on the other side where the cop had told us that people were getting ready to jump.

The smoke prevented us from seeing the people on the roof, but we sure could hear them yelling. In order to place the ladder properly, we had to lift it over a chain link fence, then we had to contend with the trees. Up the ladder I climbed as Lucky footed it. And there they were, about seven people, and they wanted to get off that roof immediately. The roof was flat and at the second floor level; a fire escape from the fourth and third floors led to the roof.

The first guy handed me a suitcase which I immediately tossed down into the trees. He then handed me a second suitcase which received the same fate. Now he had the idea—forget the suitcases and get off that roof. The first woman to get on the ladder was oriental; she was wearing a very tight, form-fitting dress. She could not get on the ladder with that tight dress. I decided I would have to help her. Using both hands, I pulled the dress up to her hips. Now she had no trouble getting on and down the ladder.

By now the windows were blowing out big time. We could hear yelling on the floor above. Lucky shoots up the fire escape and led these people down to the roof where they could take the ladder to safety.

By this time the engine company guys had water on the fire and we were holding. When it was all over, we determined we'd taken fourteen people out over ladders. As I said, *we sure could have used more men when we first arrived on the scene.* At a fire like this, the first five minutes are often all you have to get people out; the fire is spreading fast and will not wait until you call for more help. Additional apparatus often have to come from quite a distance, and unanticipated factors such as inclement weather or traffic congestion can cause delays.

The most critical engines are the ones who arrive first. It is vital that sufficient men are available; if there aren't, people, including firefighters, could die. Where life is involved, I have never known a firefighter who considered his own safety if there was a chance to save a person from a horrible death by fire. A city's or town's government must consider these facts and establish proper priorities. When the tied-together bed sheets are dangling from the window and flapping in the wind because there weren't enough firefighters to throw ladders, they will not look to the firefighters for answers and they can do their explaining to the press.

This practice of waiting for mutual aid from another city's fire department to come and supply additional help will not always work. If the other municipality is tied up with their own problems, or in situations of regional disasters such as hurricanes or blizzards, aid may be unavailable or refused. The greater the distance aid is required to travel, the more time is consumed and the likelihood of a tragedy increases.

Cities and towns need to sit down, forget their petty differences, and determine a better method of providing the people with the type of fire protection that they deserve and need.

He Was on the Pill

Chief Hally liked to have a cup of coffee with us at Lafayette Square when he picked up the morning reports. He was sitting there with his aide, watching the world come apart on television when Wally Cosidker came by and said, "Chief, will you be going near Planet Pharmacy in your travels today?"

"Sure we will, Wally. What do you need?"

"I went to see my doctor last night for a check up," Wally said, "and he gave me a few prescriptions to fill. Do you think you can take care of 'em for me?"

The aide, Eddie Feller, took the prescription, they finished their coffee, and off they went. At the pharmacy Eddie asked the pharmacist if he had an empty prescription bottle and a label. Paul, the druggist, had known Eddie and Chief Hally for years, so he provided the items. Eddie walked over to the candy counter and bought a package of multi-colored candy. Paul, somewhat bewildered, asked, "What the hell are you two up to now?"

"A little fun, Paul," the chief replied. "Just a little fun."

When they arrived at headquarters, one of the secretaries typed the following information on the label: "Take one tablet before sex to assist an erection." Eddie stuck the label on the bottle, poured some candy into the small container and re-capped the bottle. Later in the afternoon they returned to Lafayette Square and gave Wally all of his prescriptions.

The next day Wally came to work shaking his head; he seemed disturbed. "Them no good bastards!" he finally exclaimed. "I jump into bed with the old lady last night and she says, 'Wally, we got to talk. Are you keepin' anything from me?' I ask her what the hell she's talkin' about and she says, 'The pills, hon, you know the pills!' I got my mind on somethin' else and I ask her what pills. 'You know, Wally, the little bright colored pills Doctor Nelligan told you take.' Ya, Ya, Ya, I says, let's get on with it. 'Wally,' she says, 'how long've you been takin' the pills, Wally?'

"That's it—I can't take anymore. She shows me the pills. Them no good, miserable bastards!"

Chief Hally and Eddie Feller failed to show up for coffee for a few days. The damnedest thing about this prank was that we later heard Wally's wife called the doctor and asked if he thought she should take a few of the pills!

Campo Sail

There had been a multiple alarm fire at the Campo Sail Company about eighteen month previously. The structure was a two story wood frame building that ran along the railroad tracks off the Monsignor O'Brien Highway, a four—sometimes six—lane highway that runs from the Boston line to Somerville. The building's first floor contained Campo's showroom for various types of yachts, sail boats and equipment that Campo sold. The second floor was used as a furniture showroom. A loading dock ran the entire length of the building along the tracks.

When the box came in we were just putting the finishing touches on the party we were holding for Bob Harris. He was finishing up twenty-five years on Ladder 2. As usual, the cake someone's wife or friend had made was delicious. We would have ice cream and coffee. Both division chiefs and their aides had been invited. Other companies in the area would drop in later to wish Bob a happy retirement. His wife and daughters would also join us.

The department radio interrupted the festivities: "Box 1257 is being struck for report of a building fire on Monsignor O'Brien Highway near Gore Street." This area is located about two blocks from my old engine company on Second Street, so I was very familiar with the area. Fire Alarm continued: "C-2 , we are now receiving calls. The assignment will be full." Two engines, a truck and a chief would be the normal response, but due to the calls three engines, two trucks, and a heavy duty rescue would now be responding. The chief acknowledged the message. Engine 3, my old company, was in quick and ordered a working fire. On receiving this report, Fire Alarm transmitted signal 10-45 followed by the box number. An additional engine company automatically responds to this signal.

Our celebration seemed doomed. The lieutenant of Engine 2 looked at me and said, "Cap, we're out here." They were designated to cover another station. It looked like another distant covering company would be enjoying our party's homemade cake. But no! We placed it inside the hose dryer where it would be safe—we hoped—until we returned to quarters. The ice cream, however, was a problem. "Oh well," I finally said, "put it in the fridge. They can have it." With a longing last look and a shake of the head, we left the kitchen.

"C-2 calling Fire Alarm."

"Answering, C-2."

"C-2 is at the fire."

"OK, C-2, you are at the fire."

Time passes and then we hear, "C-2 to Fire Alarm." The voice is now higher pitched, quick and demanding. "On the orders of Deputy Chief Mulry, strike second alarm box 1257." This would bring two additional engine companies, another ladder truck, and the other deputy chief on duty.

"C-2 to Fire Alarm."

"Answering C-2." The aide then described to the dispatcher the type of building, obvious extent of involvement and the exposure problem.

My truck is responding on the second alarm. It is a sultry night, the kind of night when smoke refuses to rise and will hug the ground tightly like a winter blanket. We received radio orders to report to Chief Mulry in the front of the building. Chief Mulry was a cool, effective officer who knew his business. He ordered us to assist in opening up the roof. Other ladders were already up there, and a lieutenant informed me that they were encountering a false roof situation—that is, one roof added over another, and the fire was extending in between. The wind direction was not helping the situation; it was driving the fire toward the uninvolved area.

Smoke conditions were becoming real fierce and fire could be seen breaking through the roof near the loading dock. My crew had been using power saws to open up, but now the fire had gained too much headway. The section of roof under our feet was becoming spongy. When Chief Mulry was advised of the roof conditions, he immediately ordered all companies off. The fire below us now sounded like a freight train; it was really roaring. Visibility was zero, even on the roof. With great difficulty, we made our way to the aerial and descended.

We were next ordered to enter the second floor with long hooks and to pull ceilings to expose the concealed fire spreading in the area between the false roofs. Two engine companies were sent along with us to attack the fire as we opened up. We entered the building from the parking lot side. The smoke on the second floor was not too bad. Some windows had been taken out. One two and a half inch hose is advanced into the showroom, an expansive area with sofas and beds set up on both sides of the aisles. The other hose was held back as a cover line.

As Engine 5 advanced ahead of us, the feeling that something was wrong came over me. Somewhere ahead of Engine 5, a ceiling was pulled, and then there was no time to react, no time to run. We were about thirty feet into the room. There was nothing but fire in front of the facepiece of my Scott air mask. I felt my body being picked up by a searing hot force and blown through a swinging door. Fred Iser was on top of me. He went over my head. We were against a wall in the hallway. Fred's mask was off and he was stunned. The smoke had risen and I could see the front of the stairs.

At this point, we rolled down the stairs and out the door. The smoke was on the ground again. We crawled across the asphalt parking lot until my hand touched what felt like a pair of boots. I followed the boots up the form, looked up and saw the face of Father Mahoney, the Boston Fire Department's chaplain. "Hi, Father," I said. "Good to see ya!" Fred was sitting there, still a little dazed, his rubber coat smoking. Someone began examining my neck and ears. The cool of the stretcher felt wonderful against my back. Chief Mulry stood there looking at me. "What happened to the engine crews that were up there with us?" I asked. He told me that the fire blew over their heads and that the crew had used the line to cover themselves as they made their retreat.

I lay on my stomach in the emergency room of the Mass. General Hospital in Boston. Fred was on the next table and they were really working on him. I could hear them talking about his lungs. His mask was blown from his face in the backdraft. A cute nurse poured something over my head, neck and ears. It felt cool. I gave her a wink and got a wink in return.

When they were finally done with me, I looked like a mummy. Fred was held for a possible concussion and burns to the face. A chief's car picked me up and took me to Engine 2 and Ladder 3's quarters. When I arrived home I hesitated in front of the house. I knew that seeing me like this, all wrapped in bandages, would distress Peggy. I hoped the kids were all in bed. When Peggy opened the door for me she said, "Hi, hon, I have a cup of coffee for you. Bobby called and said you were on your way home." I still believe that the soldiers who wait at home are real and true heroes.

To Smell So Good

I remember a blind man named Eddie who lived in the neighborhood and used to hang around Engine 2 and Ladder 3's house. Out of the blue this one firefighter started to complain that wherever he goes, there Eddie is right behind him. He sits down for a cup coffee and boom—Eddie is always there beside him. Bob told the guy the reason Eddie was following him was his after-shave lotion. This the guy refused to believe. Bob said he would prove it and sprinkled some of the complainer's after-shave on the patrol desk.

Later in the day Eddie came into quarters and walked over and started talking to the empty desk. Now the guy was a believer. Later when we told Eddie about the experiment, he got a big laugh out of it.

Whenever we had a meal, Eddie was always invited; we were very good friends. One cold and snowy night we had a working fire about five blocks from the station. Eddie showed up with a bag of doughnuts. He had walked down to the fire, slipping and sliding on the ice, to be with us. There were hose lines all over the street and sidewalk. For the life of us we never could figure out how he made it. He later told me that he followed the sound of the pumping engine and the smell of the smoke.

What the Lord takes away he will in some way replace.

A Little Gas If You Please

Whenever I see one of those ads for "Classic Music of the 70s" on TV, I can only think of gas rationing and long lines at gas stations! *That* was the 70s. There was just no gas around.

At the time I was captain of Engine 2 in Lafayette Square. We received a call one afternoon from Fire Alarm to investigate an odor of gas on the third floor of a building on Massachusetts Avenue. When we arrived at the building we were met by a guy who informed us that gasoline is coming through the ceiling on the third floor. Unbelievable, but gasoline *is* dripping over a large area of the floor. This building is a second class structure, i.e. brick and wood construction, and this floor was used as a disco dance hall and bar. The first floor was being used as a bike repair shop, the second as offices and the fourth floor was supposedly vacant. I notified Fire Alarm to dispatch a ladder truck to assist in evacuation and forcible entry, and also to notify the police.

We forced the door on the fourth floor and found approximately thirty 55 gallon drums of gasoline stored illegally; at least four of the drums are rusted out and leaking. This building was in our inspection district, and this floor had been found vacant the last time we looked it over.

The division chief responded and all proper authorities were notified. When Fire Prevention caught up to the owner, he claimed that he was "doing a favor for a friend" and never realized the danger. His friend apparently owned a local taxi businesses, and without gas he was finished.

If the building had been occupied with dancers, we could have had a real "Disco Inferno." This is the same building that I received a complaint about from a citizen suggesting that we should look closely at the sprinkler system a month earlier. I did and found that the system was nothing more than heads stuck on the ceiling. Some people are dangerously stupid.

A Skid on a Bridge

It was a cold, raw, windy night, the kind of miserable night when you hope that you can stay in.

The call came in about 3:00 a.m. for a car that went off the Harvard Bridge and into the Charles River. Engine 2 and Ladder 3 responded. We were located about three blocks away and arrived at the scene quickly. The truck was the first to arrive and I reported to the deputy. He was looking down at the ice and said, "Captain, believe it or not we have two cars down there. " One car had hit the ice head on and the part showing was the trunk; the rest was under the water. Another car was also down on the ice; it was on its back about thirty yards away. The ice had cracked all around and the car was in a pool of water. There were no signs of life anywhere down there.

The Harvard Bridge (commonly, though incorrectly, called the "Mass. Ave. Bridge") connects Cambridge and Boston with a four lane highway. It had snowed heavily the day before and there were snow banks along the sides. Both cars must have hit the banks, climbed up, then flew over the rail and dropped about thirty feet to the ice below.

We pulled a forty-five foot ladder, tied the pawls, and lowered it over the rail to the river. I climbed down to the ice; it felt solid. Keeping the line around my waist, I started to crawl toward the car that was through the ice. I still saw no sign of life. The wind was really whipping down on the river. They were yelling something from above, but I couldn't make it out. Walter Lane, the lieutenant on the Rescue, was beside me now.

They were lowering a twenty-foot straight wall ladder to us. Joe Jenkins, Walter and I slid the aluminum ladder across the hole.

At that moment an occupant of the car broke the surface of the water along side the trunk. Joe had gone around to the far side of the hole and we slid the ladder to the trunk. I tried to ask the guy if anybody else was in the car but he wouldn't answer me. Walter, who was lighter than I, climbed out on the ladder and got the guy. When we pulled him on the ice Walter said, "Check him for bleeding," and the guy yelled out, "I wasn't speeding!" Guess he still had water in his ears. He then told us that no one else was in the car, which made us very happy since by now the thing was sinking fast. We tied him in a stokes litter and they pulled him up to the bridge.

I never saw the operation with the other car. They told me later that three guys were found unconscious inside. That must have been a hairy rescue—the car sank just as they removed the last victim.

We later heard from the Metropolitan Police that one car was chasing the other from the Roxbury section of Boston—some drug related dispute. They were all very lucky. They could have been at the bottom of the Charles.

Take the Car in Town

The still alarm was for a car on fire on Memorial Drive, a kind of parkway that runs along the Cambridge side of the Charles River. Engine 2 and Ladder 3 responded. It was a flat-bed truck with crushed cars on it. The truck, however, was not supposed to be Memorial Drive, which is for passenger cars exclusively. We ran the booster line and operated—no good. Now we ran a one and a half inch line. Still no good.

Now I was getting angry. Just then one of my men called my attention to the fact that the river is on fire. I have a magnesium engine burning and flowing down the gutter and into the river. Great! Magnesium is lighter than water; it will float on the surface. Water was not the answer. Send more police for traffic. Send sand from the city yard. Send in the Marines.

We were now getting the upper hand. We threw shovelful after shovelful on the burning mass. The fire was finally going out. I felt someone tugging on my coat, turned and heard, "Hey, Captain, you know that piece of burning metal? Well, it floated under the boat house dock and...well now the dock's on fire."

Strike the box for a fire in a boat house full of expensive rowing sculls and boats. We used forcible entry tools to gain access to the boat house. It's full of smoke. A working fire. "Shit!" I yell and then I hear, "Hey, Captain, that flat-bed trailer is goin' again."

I begin to give orders to my men and tell the driver to take his goddam truck to the next bridge and cross the river.

"Why?" he asks.

"Because they're not as busy as us at the moment. That's why."

The final results: the small fire under the pier was extinguished; I stepped on a nail and had to go to the hospital for a tetanus shot; one of my men fell into the river and had to be rescued.

The last we saw of the flat-bed truck with the crushed cars, it was crossing the Mass. Ave. bridge toward Boston—in a ball of fire.

The Organ

"Don't hit the organ!" The Reverend Doctor Kinsey was glaring at the deputy chief. "Don't hit the organ—it came to this country on the first ship that landed after the *Mayflower*."

The chief spoke softly but with a commanding voice: "Reverend, there is smoke coming from it and I'm afraid we cannot find another source," as he thinks to himself, My first day in the chief's car and I have to run into a winner.

"I don't care, do you hear? I know you firemen! You crawl into people's windows and break up furniture with those big axes you carry."

The chief decided it was going to be a long day.

The call had come in for a fire in Lord's Church in Harvard Square. The chief had a full response—three engines, two trucks and himself. He has sufficient help...if he can only find where the damned smoke is coming from. Lord's is a large wood church that dates back to the eighteenth century. Walking away from the reverend, the chief puts his arm around the captain of Engine 1 and says, "For the love of Christ, Larry, this guy is on my case! Did we look everywhere?"

"Yes we did, Chief. There's only a trace of smoke now, but it does seem to have come from the organ. Here he comes again, Chief."

"Mister Fireman, I am warning you for the last time...leave my organ alone."

The lieutenant of the ladder truck reported that he has checked the first floor and the cellar; both are clear. Slowly all helmeted figures turn in the direction of the ornate wooden organ. Could it be that someone had dropped a cigarette down inside?

"I repeat, sir, spare my organ."

Enough is enough, thinks the chief, but he says, "Reverend, please remember that we did not invite ourselves in here. You called us. Now will you please let us do our job."

"Chief, the damned organ is smoking again," someone says. Now the smoke can be seen. It is curling in the air currents as it rises from the top of the beautiful hand carved keyboard. The reverend has returned to the chief's side. He is shaking his head; he is getting ready to cry. "Reverend, have we looked everywhere? Let's go down to the cellar."

"Very well, Chief, but you must remember, *that* instrument is irreplaceable."

As they gaze around the cellar the chief says, "Now *think*, Reverend! Are there any rooms that are concealed that the men may have missed?"

The minister is shaking his sad face, then suddenly his eyes brighten: "Yes! There is a tomb! And you know, Chief, that area is right beneath the organ."

Now we're getting hot. The engine crew had been standing by with the pipe in a bucket near the organ so no water would drip on the floor. Ladder 1's crew are standing there with their axes poised, waiting for the order to play a few chords on the organ. The custodian arrives with a large iron ring with large iron keys. As he unlocks the door, he says, "No one has been in here in years." The large metal door is now swinging open. Inside the air is cold and damp. There are no lights in here. The chief begins searching the ceiling with his Wheat light. There it is, under the organ, an old electric motor that somehow started to run again. It had overheated and caused the old wooden beams to char, thus the smoke.

Cambridge Electric is notified, and they are requested to have an inside service crew respond to the church. The engine crew wets down the charred area. The chief notifies Fire Alarm that he would hold one engine for awhile; he dismisses all other apparatus from the scene.

This is a tomb. Gravestones were piled against the foundation wall. Now that the reverend knew his precious organ would not fall under the axeman's pounding hatchet, his temperament changed for the better. Knowing that he was going to stay a bit longer, the chief asked about the tomb and a story was told.

Reverend Kinsey said that even before the Revolutionary War the dead were buried beneath the church in order to prevent grave robbers from stealing from the dead. The custodian had by now provided a candle and the flickering light cast dark shadows against the gravestones. Although most people in Cambridge supported the Revolution, the town did have a few Tories, people who remained loyal to the British Crown, mostly affluent people who stood to lose a lot if the Revolution succeeded. "These graves contained many of the aristocrats who had lived on Brattle Street," said the reverend. The chief walked deeper into the dark and musty graveyard under the wooden church floor. His light fell on a granite tomb with a small stone seat and table.

"What is that?" asks the chief. Reverend Kinsey is now at his side and relates the story to the firefighter: In the third year of the Revolution, the city of Cambridge seemed an occupied town; British troops were even camping on the Common. A young British officer fell in love with the seventeen year old daughter of a prominent Tory family who lived on Brattle Street. On moonlit nights they would walk the cobblestoned paths and plan a life together onces these bothersome rebels were silenced.

Their love was as real as the soft odor of lilac that hung from the bushes along the way. Happiness, however, was not to be. There was another young officer in the regiment who also vied for the affection of the young maiden. One night in a tavern, as the dimness of the flickering candle foretold the tragic events to follow, it all came to an end. Hot words were exchanged between the two officers and sabers were drawn. The combatants took positions in the rear yard of the tavern. A full Harvest Moon was hidden by the dark clouds of anger. Her lover, the handsome young lieutenant who had walked beside her, lay dead on the fallen leaves.

He was buried in the tomb under the church. She never married and spent much of her life sitting in the dampness where wilted lilacs had been placed on the table. She was buried as she wished, beside her love.

The reverend's voice trailed off.

The crew foreman from Cambridge Electric said that it was obvious that electrical work had been done recently and that somehow a motor that operated an old venting fan had become activated. The Reverend Kinsey thanked everyone involved and the chief requested the all out be sounded.

The chief never forgot the incident, and each time he drives past the church he swears he could smell fresh lilacs.

Benny the Match

She kept saying it over and over again, "Oh, what a lovely fire!" To me it looked like any other job. Heavy fire was showing from the windows of a second floor apartment in a housing project. Fires in this type of structure are rather routine. These buildings are first class construction, and a fire will usually be confined to the apartment of origin.

It was a rather hot summer night August. The smoke was hanging very, very low, making ventilation very difficult. I was acting deputy chief in Division Two. The box came in about 7:00 p.m. When I arrived, companies were already advancing lines inside. Ladder 3 had its stick to the roof and was working to open the roof door above the stairs.

I was standing in front of the building and I guess that she didn't know who I was. My aide, John Hathaway, had just reported to me by portable radio that they had water on the fire and were making good progress. "Gee that's a swell fire, don't you think, mister?" she said. About this time I had enough of her admiring the "lovely fire." As I moved away from her she said, "Benny the Match—he do a good job, mister." Now I stopped dead in my tracks and up went my ears. Moving closer to her I replied, "Yeah, Benny the Match does do a good job. It *is* quite a fire!"

The woman still didn't have the foggiest idea to whom she was speaking. "Mrs. Semerlis told me about him. He work very cheap. I try for two months to get him, but he worth the wait. He no answer the telephone if he no know you, I guess. Mrs.

Domminie, she tell him I OK to talk to."

My aide was now calling me about one of my men who was badly cut. I moved away from my talkative friend and made sure that an ambulance was at the scene. It was Larry Cummings from Ladder 2; he had a badly lacerated wrist, just above the glove line.

The arson investigator, Firefighter Louder, was at the scene. My lady was still there, still telling anyone who would listen what a fine fire it was. Investigator Louder took out his little notebook and asked if she would mind if he took some notes. She asked him he would like a fire too. He simply replied that he'd be grateful if she would tell him all her about her friend, Benny the Match.

The fire was knocked down and I started to make up some of the companies. After sending in the all out signal, we went to the Cambridge City Hospital to inquire about Larry. They were just finishing stitching him up; it took eight stitches to close the wound. As we sat in the waiting room, I could not help but notice the people who sat there waiting to be treated. Some were obviously poor. Some seemed strung out on dope. A young man with a little girl on his lap nervously waited to be seen. The girl was about four years old and seemed very sick. Her mother sat beside her and held her head. A police officer had a young man in hall who did not like handcuffs. The man had a welt on his cheek that needed medical attention. His jaw was probably fractured.

We drove Larry back to Ladder 2's quarters. He was placed off duty and went home. I returned to the division office and put in a call to the Fire Investigation Unit. The report that Eddie Louder gave me was, to say the least, incredible. According to my fire admirer, there was an agency that would replace all home furnishings that were destroyed by a fire. She also said that Benny was paid twenty-five dollars for his work. Many of her friends in the housing project had used Benny. The waiting period for his services was about four months because he was so busy.

It was later determined that Benny the Match was working in at least three cities. Benny the Match was extinguished and pleaded no contest. When the judge asked him why he did such a thing, he replied, "Your honor, I provide a good service cheap."

Even today as I drive by that building, now all boarded up, I think of Benny the Match and a smile comes to my lips.

A Sunday Among the Stones

It was one of those stunningly beautiful early spring days that have a taste of summer about them. The regular chief was off duty and I was assigned to cover Division One. Although assigned to a regular company, occasionally a captain is detailed to cover for a deputy chief. My aide was George Thomson, and we were looking forward to a nice quiet day. After we visited all the stations in the division and picked up the daily reports, we decided to cruise around a bit.

George asked me if I had ever been inside Mount Auburn Cemetery. He said that it was truly beautiful this time of year. It's located at the edge of our district and I saw no reason why we couldn't enjoy the splendor of the morning, so I replied, "Let's go."

Mount Auburn is a very large cemetery with many streets and paths. George was right: the flowers, shrubs, bushes, and trees were magnificent. On we drove in total peace and pleasure. Then the radio came alive, first a warning tone then the words, "Box 6521 is being struck for abuilding fire. OK C-3." "C-3 has the box," I replied, then turned to George and said, "Let's go."

We had one small problem, however. How do we get out of here? No siren, no lights until we hit the street. What street? Where the hell is the way out? Up one and down another, they all seemed to go in a circle. It was early Sunday morning and there was no one around.

"Fire Alarm to C-3."

"C-3," I answer.

"Chief, we are now receiving calls."

I groan loudly. Don't panic—George is doing his best. We are now driving over grass. It is spring and the earth is soft and I am soft for being in here...and we are now stuck in the mud. On the radio I hear, "Engine 9 to Fire Alarm, heavy fire showing."

"OK, Engine 9. You are reporting heavy fire showing. OK, C-3?" Fire Alarm asks.

I groan silently and reply, "C-3 has the message."

About this time I am seriously thinking of taking the portable, jumping a fence and calling a cab. My head is spinning—so are the wheels. Just when I am about to call us out of service and have us covered by the other division, George is able to get us back on the road. But where does the damned road go?

I see the gate and we make for it. On the real street, lights on, siren on, we are rolling at last. When I finally arrive at the scene, Captain Lang of Engine 8 reports that it was a kitchen fire and it's been knocked down. Someone was cooking their bacon. For awhile I thought my bacon was cooked. Companies overhauled and removed debris.

No one ever asked me where I was. I have always said that a good officer is a reflection of his good crew. Members of the fire service work as a team; the men are professionals who know what must be done and they will do it. A good working company goes to work on the fire and does not necessarily wait for the orders of a chief officer. After all, he might be delayed.

All Stuck in the Mud

Another beautiful mid-spring Sunday morning. I always loved this time of year; the ice is finally out of the ground, the earth is soft, things are starting to grow again.

At this time I was acting deputy chief of Division 2, which is all of North Cambridge, from Harvard Square to the Belmont-Arlington line. While picking morning reports at the various firehouses, I received a radio call from Fire Alarm informing me that the lieutenant of an engine company wanted to see me. They were at a still alarm at the Arthur D. Lawrence complex. This large research complex is located on Route 2 near the Belmont line. The engine company had gone up there for a small brush fire. The lieutenant told me that there was a brush fire down by the brook; however, the area was very difficult to reach. The fire was spreading with the wind and heading toward some buildings. This area is marsh land and extends for a quite a distance behind the complex. In order to keep the lay short and get maximum pressure on the line, he positioned the hose wagon as close as he safely could.

The fire was now out, but we were about to lose a $125,000 fire engine because it was stuck in the mud. We decided to bring the pump down as close as possible, but still on firm ground, to pull the hose wagon out with a cable. Good idea, yes? Well, no actually because now the pump was also stuck and sinking fast. I had wanted this to be a good day.

Now I notified Fire Alarm to have the other chief cover the division; I also requested that they dispatch the Heavy Duty Rescue Company to the scene. When they arrived I ordered them to stay up on the road and use their cable winch to pull everybody free. The hose wagon was tilting toward the creek, and I started to wish that I had called in sick on this beautiful mid-spring Sunday morning.

The boys did a good job of cutting down trees and making a corduroy road. Everything was ready for the winch...we would finally be out of there...right? Wrong. Due to the angle of pull, the Heavy Duty Rescue rig slid on the wet leaves and joined the rest of the Cambridge Fire Department—stuck in the mud of a marsh near the Belmont line. About this time I told my aide to call me a cab; I was going home with a headache.

Then someone, I can't remember who, suggested we try to get the services of a large wheeled tractor kept at the city yard. I called Fire Alarm and asked them to see what they could do. The called back and said the tractor was on the way.

While we were waiting we off-loaded all the heavy equipment carried on the Rescue unit; the other pieces were already stripped. When the tractor driver arrived, he scratched his head and said this was the damnedest thing that he had ever seen. I had to agree.

Hooking a chain onto the Rescue, he started to pull and I started to pray. The large tires on the tractor did the trick; up the hill came Rescue onto firm ground. Next came the pumper; up, up it came and we all applauded. Now the hose wagon. The tractor operator studied the situation, then looked at me and said, "Chief, we have one shot. If it don't work I think we'll lose the tractor and the wagon. I know this area—this is all quicksand kind of marsh and the creek is about twenty feet deep."

The chain was attached to the shackle. The wagon was listing badly and going down bow first. I felt that my career was going with it. A strain was taken...praise the Lord! she was moving up, up, and then the hose wagon came onto the bank. We were saved. I more than thanked the tractor operator and handed him a twenty, which he refused and which I stuck in his shirt pocket.

We cleaned up everything, and except for a few dents and scratches, all was well. On the way home that night I went to church and thanked God for pulling my career out of the marshlands of north, North Cambridge.

A House Full of Flame

My time as a member of the Cambridge Fire Department was coming to a close. The date for my retirement was set—February 4, 1993. This would finish off forty-two years on the job. I'd had, I thought, a long and fruitful career, but the happiest years were those spent as a snotty-nose hose man. With rank comes responsibility. The years that I spent riding the rear step of Engine 5's hose wagon, hanging on to the deck, held fond memories for me. We would follow the pump down Cambridge Street, the sirens blaring. My back was to the direction we were going and I couldn't care less. I was enjoying the ride.

Years later when I was promoted to the rank of deputy chief, my new assignment was at fire headquarters. I was placed in charge of property; my official title was Director of Support Services. This meant that I was in charge of seeing that, among other things, proper amounts of supplies were assigned to each company. On the night of the huge 1975 fireworks display on the Charles River, I was assigned to cover the Division One car. Bob Clancy, acting lieutenant of Engine 7, notified me that he had an emergency in quarters. There was a line of people outside the firehouse that was three blocks long; every single soul in the line wanted to use the bathrooms in the firehouse. The supply of toilet paper, of course, had been exhausted. Some of the women in line were threatening Acting Lieutenant Clancy with bodily harm if the tissue did not start to roll again. I didn't want anyone to raise a stink about the issue, so I decided we'd better get the house some tissue. We obtained three large boxes from supply and delivered them to the station. Everyone was relieved.

When I answered the phone first thing in the morning, few people would start the conversation with "How was your night, Chief?" Instead, they would ask if I knew that someone kicked in the door of engine whatever? or did I know that someone stole the telephone booth from in front of quarters? Sometimes I thought the job seemed almost exclusively negative. I knew it was a helluva long way from riding the back of Engine 5.

When Chief Engineer Kevin Fitzgerald came into my office one morning and asked me if I wanted to take a division for awhile before I retired, I jumped at the opportunity. Kevin and I had worked on the line together. He stands in my book as one of the finest persons I've ever known on the job.

This was to be my last tour of duty in the car. Division One is East Cambridge and the more active division. My old aide, John Hathaway, was assigned as my driver. I met the car at Engine 9's quarters. It was good to see John again. When my wife Peggy was in the hospital dying of cancer in 1987, I was assigned as acting deputy of Division 2; John was my driver during this time, and we became very close friends. All the guys with whom I worked were very supportive. When I was working days in the Division 2 car, the chief of department gave me permission to spend some time with Peg. John would stay with the car in front of the hospital while I went up to Peggy's room. If he wanted me, he would call me on the portable radio. The Division One chief would cover both districts. Peg would ask, "What are you doing here, hon?" "It's OK, Peg, I have permission." She would just gently shake her head. That was a sad time in my life. Peggy and I were married for thirty-two years and had seven children. We'd had a good life together and now....

The early part of the evening was on the quiet side. We had the usual false alarms pulled. At about 7:00 p.m. John said that the boys at Engine 5, my old station, had planned a party for me. We were also due at a party at Engine 2 and Ladder 3. I was starting to feel like a social butterfly. Since Division 2 puts up at Engine 5's quarters, we decided to make that the last stop.

On the way we stopped by Engine 3 and Ladder 2. I had been stationed there as a captain. We had a cup of coffee with them.

The next stop was Lafayette Square. They were waiting for us. I've seen plenty of party cakes during my time on the department, but Engine 2 and Ladder 3 outdid them all. It was red, white and blue with a frosting picture of an engine and a ladder pulling out of quarters; the scene had cars and street signs and many more small details. Three of my sons were there, Michael, Neal and Timmy. Mike and Neal are firefighters in Nashua, New Hampshire. Timmy is a motorcycle cop in Cambridge.

Pictures were taken and a good time was had by all. We had roast beef, potato salad, rolls, chips and dips, the whole works. Different companies in the division dropped by. Some of the old timers with whom I worked over the years stopped in to say hello and to wish me well. The uptown deputy and his aide stopped by, had some cake, and told me that they would cover our division. There was no indication of what the night had reserved for us.

At about eleven we finally returned to Engine 5. They had also been waiting for us. Yes, another party, this time it was deli meats, cheeses, ravioli and chianti. Of course, there was also another cake, but calmer heads prevailed and we decided to wait on the cake.

It was 2:18 a.m. on January 14, 1993. I lay there in bed and could not sleep. The cold wind was rattling the windows. Maybe my sleepless state had something to do with those wonderful hot Italian sausages I'd eaten. Maybe it was the excitement of the last night in the car. When the house lights came up and the tone started, it was almost as if I knew it was about to happen. As we ran toward the sliding pole, Fire Alarm was announcing the box: "Striking box 2851 for a building fire on Prospect Street." Running beside me for the pole was Bobby Quinn, acting lieutenant of Engine 5. He said to me, "Chief, I could feel this coming. We have a fire!"

John was already in the car. Fire Alarm was calling me on the radio: "Fire Alarm calling C-2."

"C-2 answering," I replied.

"Chief, we are getting calls for people trapped in the

building." I acknowledged the information and as we started out the door, I looked at the clock above the patrol desk. It was 2:20 a.m.

It was snowing as we turned right onto Hampshire Street. The road was a little slick. Staring through the windshield wipers John said to me, "Connie, we've got a fire." We turned right onto Prospect and I remember thinking, My last night in the car and I get a fire! John was now pulling over toward the curb. I pick up the mike and told Fire Alarm that I was on scene; John was already running toward the building. As he ran he yelled to me that we had heavy smoke showing. I was almost in front of the building and I could see not only heavy smoke, but also a sight that I will long remember—people were hanging out of the second and third floor windows.

As I ran up the driveway next to the house, I slipped on the ice and landed on my back. My helmet fell off, but I still had the portable mike in my hand. Looking to my left I could see into the cellar. It was heavily involved in fire. "C-2 to Fire Alarm." They acknowledged. "On the order of Deputy Chief O'Brien, strike a second alarm and give me another truck company." Normally a second alarm would have given me two more engine companies and another ladder company, but due to the obvious extent of the fire and the severe life hazard, I would need that additional ladder truck. You could say that I ordered my last multiple while laying on my back!

With the amount of fire in the cellar and the heavy smoke conditions on the upper floors, it was quite apparent that the fire had run the walls. This was a three story frame dwelling measuring about sixty by forty feet. The roof was of mansard type construction, i.e. a roof having two slopes on all sides with the lower slope almost vertical and the upper slope almost horizontal. When I regained my feet I called Fire Alarm and advised them of the severe life hazard and extension of the fire. I also told them to have the first truck company bring a thirty-five foot ladder to the right rear of the building.

When we arrived, Engine 5 was right behind us. Bob Quinn, Five's acting lieutenant, was a well-seasoned firefighter. He reported to me with a two and a half inch line to protect the people using the rear egress. They were just tumbling out the

—223—

door. John was pulling people out the rear door and keeping the exit clear for others. Engine 2 arrived about the same time and I ordered them to advance a big line to cover the front door. Ladder 3 was the first truck to arrive; it was commanded by Acting Lieutenant Dan Maloney, a seasoned and efficient firefighter. Using a thirty-five foot ground ladder, Ladder 3 started to evacuate people out of the second and third floor windows. Rescue 1 arrived and started a search of the second and third floors.

We later determined that members of the Cambridge Fire Department rescued seventeen people from that building; many more managed to get out on their own. The place was simply loaded with people. An inquiry revealed the building was inhabited primarily by Hispanic immigrants—not all of them possessing the proper documentation for being in the United States. Beds were found in the basement.

The fire now had control of all floors and was headed for the roof. As the various companies arrived and went to work, they were reporting to me that there was fire extending in all directions. I requested a third alarm and notified Fire Alarm of conditions. The temperature was twelve degrees above zero and it was snowing hard. Multiple alarm units would encounter dangerous road conditions.

Fire was now blowing out the second and third floor windows on the left side of the building. We had an exposure problem on that side. The adjacent building was of the same height and of similar construction. Only about fifteen feet of space separated the two structures. The wind was blowing at a moderate speed...in that direction. Big lines were ordered into the alley between the structures. I was standing in the alley on the exposure side when I heard someone calling, "Deputy O'Brien! Deputy O'Brien!" As I turned toward the front of the building, I saw what they were concerned about. Heavy fire was overlapping out the front door. The front of the place was a complete sheet of ice; men were slipping and sliding as they moved lines to counter the new exposure. The ladder men were having great difficulty throwing ground ladders because of the slope of the driveway.

An officer in the front told me that he believed that the Rescue

Company had gone up the front stairs. When I called Rescue to advise them about the stairs, the captain told me they were trapped in the second floor hallway and trying to get to the front windows. Just then Engine 7 called me, yelling that they were trapped on the third floor rear—and that a member was missing. There'd been a serious backdraft and the fire was rapidly gaining headway.

I ordered a ladder placed to the second floor front window. The chief in command at the rear had also heard the "May Day" and had dispatched an engine company to advance a support line to cover Engine 7. Even now I can remember the feeling that come over me. My mind was racing and I can remember thinking, Oh my God, on my last night of fire duty I have men trapped and missing. I was breaking out in a cold sweat, regardless of the frigid temperature. My knees became weak and I started trembling. The image of walking behind a funeral procession flashed through my mind. I had taken off my gloves to work the mike, and my fingers were now numb from the cold. I couldn't tell if the key was depressed or not. I put my hand into the pocket of my turnout coat to warm it, but that didn't help at all.

Rescue was at the front window. Heavy black smoke was starting to push out the second floor windows. There was going to be another explosion. I ordered a big line to cover the front of the building. They were now knocking down the heavy fire blowing out the front door. One by one the Rescue members came out of the window. The first man slid down the snow-covered roof to the tip of the ground ladder, and the others followed. The captain was the last one out. They all had made it. No sooner had the captain made it to the ladder than the entire room lit up. Now heavy fire was blowing out two windows. The chief in command of the rear called me and told me that Engine 7 had made it out safely—but a member was still missing.

When I arrived at the rear of the building, the chief told me that search companies were looking for the man, but they were being hampered by heavy fire conditions. I ordered two more engine companies and another truck company to the fire. I also ordered all interior firefighting to cease and all members not actively engaged in searching operations to evacuate the building. Each company officer would take a roll call and report any missing members to me. Metro Fire has an adopted procedure for this situation: when an incident commander orders a roll call of all firefighting personnel, apparatus at the scene will simultaneously sound their horns. The reason for this is that in some cases, because of the intensity of the fire, it might be difficult for a man to hear the radio alert signal to evacuate.

The fire was now coming through the roof and shooting about thirty feet high. The crews on the lee of the fire were doing a good job of covering the exposures. Finally, after what felt like an eternity, the result of the roll call was relayed to me. All members were accounted for—the missing man from Engine 7 had been located. He reported that he was the last one on the line when it blew and a section of the ceiling came down on top of him. He was knocked into a rear room and had to untangle himself from debris. There was a ladder in the window, so he evacuated to the rear yard. In the confusion he ended up working with another company and was totally unaware that anyone was looking for him. At a later date I would make it a point of having a discussion with this firefighter concerning the importance of accountability...but for the moment I was overjoyed to see him.

The heavy appliances had done their job. Fresh engine companies could now advance a safe distance into the building and put water on the residual fire. It was becoming daylight. The snow had finally stopped, but everything was covered with ice. This is a tough time at a cold job. The body has slowed down and now the cold really sets in. Wet clothes become ice water against the skin. I realized that I had to go to the bathroom in the worst way. I made my way inside the burnt-out first floor and found a bathroom. As I stood there relieving myself the thought that this night was approaching its end came to me and I was happy for it. The Salvation Army was at the scene with hot coffee for the men. The public works department sanded the area and walking was becoming less hazardous. I sure wished I had worn heavy wool socks. My feet felt like two blocks of ice. When I walked I could hear the crunch of the snow beneath my boots, but I could not feel my feet.

I was standing out in front of the building when Chief Engineer Fitzgerald approached me. "Well, Connie," he said, "you had your final fire."

"Yes, sir, I sure did, and I thank you very much."

A broad smile came over his Irish face and he said, "Wrap it up, Connie. Your relief is here."

I advised the day chief where the mop-up lines were and which companies had already been dismissed. As I walked back to the car I noticed that the doughnut shop on the corner of Broadway and Prospect Street was open. The owner had heard about the fire and come to work early. Sitting inside were people with white blankets over their heads. At a later time the union would present the owner with a plaque.

John rubbed his hands together and started the car. "Well, Chief, it was quite a night!" he said.

"Yes, John, it was quite interesting," I replied.

The traffic on Broadway was getting heavy. It was the start of another day in the City of Cambridge.

The Last Day

I didn't sleep well, and when the alarm clock went off, I was already awake. Mary said, "It's time to get up, hon."

It was to be my last day on the job, and Kevin told me to wear my dress uniform to work. When I arrived at headquarters, he was already there. While we had a cup of coffee in his office, he told me that we were going to the Metro Fire Chiefs' meeting. This is a monthly meeting of the over twenty fire department chiefs whose cities and towns comprise the metropolitan Boston area. At about ten o'clock, Kevin came into my office and told me to get my hat and coat. The meeting was to be held at a school in Newton, MA, which is about a twenty minute drive from Cambridge. There was a large crowd at the meeting; I'd rarely seen so much brass in one place. Coffee and doughnuts were available. A new mobile Metro Fire Command Center was parked in the school yard and we all had a tour of the facility. It contained all the latest radio equipment, and I wondered how we ever managed to put out fires without it.

We left the meeting at about eleven-thirty and headed back towards Cambridge. The only trouble was that Kevin was taking me on a cook's tour of Boston. He was also always driving in the inside lane; baby carriages were passing us. We talked about the old days. I told him I could remember his first day on the job. He was appointed shortly after his discharge from the Marine Corps. We worked together at Engine 5 and saw plenty of action. One of the more memorable fires was the Squires. Kevin was one of the crew who helped pull me out from under a deck gun.

When we finally reached headquarters, I saw the reason for the stall. They had a cake and the whole works waiting for me. Deli platters, salads, rolls—the table was loaded with food. The girls in the office had outdone themselves. My son, Timmy, the Cambridge motorcycle cop, was there and some of the old gang from Engine 5.

At about 1 p.m., Kevin called me to the outer office and called Fire Alarm on the radio. He told them that at this time, until eighteen hundred hours, I was Acting Chief of Department. He then handed me the C-1 radio and went home.

The girls took over now. We struck a pose for photos—me with a large cigar in my mouth and two girls on my lap. I promoted two firefighters to the rank of lieutenant; one had recently been suspended and the other was in the process of resigning because he did not like smoke. I then granted each of the three secretaries a fifty dollar a week raise. We did have some fun.

Soon it was time to go home. I took my box of personal things and one last look around and closed the door. Left there forever was a little piece of my heart. I did not look back.

The All Out is in!